RONDA

"*Dreamed City*" and the Serranía

by José Páez Carrascosa

*Dedicated
to Sergio and Victoria Eugenia*

C O L L A B O R A T I O N S

T R A N S L A T I O N	Mrs. Katie Boyle
P R O L O G U E	Professore Michele Antonucci
P I C T U R E S	Don J. Agustín Núñez - Edilux
	Don Daniel Nuñez Caballero
D R A W I N G S	Dña. Cinta Roca Pulido
M A Q U E T T E - M A K E R	Don Germán Madinabeitia Peiró

M Y   S I N C E R E   T H A N K S   T O :

Sra. Dña. Aurora Miró

Sra. Dña. Isabel López Infante

Rvdo. Don Gonzalo Huesa Lope

Don Miguel Martín Pinzón

Don Salvador Ordóñez "Cuso"

Don Diego Martín Narváez

Don Rafael Aguilera Hormigo

Don Bartolomé Nieto González

Don Manuel Bellido García

2ª Edición
© ALL RIGHTS RESERVED
RONDA EDITORIAL
C/. INFANTES, 67 - RONDA
DEPÓSITO LEGAL: GR - 1167 - 1996
I.S.B.N.: 84 - 922176 - 3 - 4
FOTOMECÁNICA: FRANACOLOR
IMPRIME: COPARTGRAF

I N D E X

Picture by Kurt Hielscher. 1918

P R O L O G U E

Don José Páez Carrascosa is Rondan and simply (and proudly?) as he declares in the introduction to the preceding edition of his "Guide", Rondan to the core. He loves Ronda so passionately that when he comments on its beauty, its heroic deeds or its misfortunes, he set himself on fire with fantasy and his words acquire a breath of air that fascinates, and thanks to the contained emotion, the history and geography of Ronda are no longer dull information; instead they reach the tone of a short epic.

Perhaps, because of this love, he has taken the decision to guide tourists through his home town, carrying out this activity with care, accuracy, courtesy and enthusiasm. I sensed this myself when, during a visit to Ronda, after having listened to him for two hours I was obliged to feel great esteem for him. Also, whoever reads this book will notice, with what clarity and purity of expression, with what command, minuteness and richness of information the landscapes, artistic treasures and the peculiarities of Ronda unfold before our eyes, and how the past is brought back to life along the tracks of the present, with instinctive and loving eloquence.

But our author is, what´s more, a cultured person and amongst other things he has attended the Italian University for foreigners in Perugia. Because of his passion for study he has wanted to check information given in the previous edition of his "Guide" and has discovered that some statements commonly believed to be indisputable are not acceptable and therefore he has corrected them. Also, bravely facing costs and editorial risks he has filled voids and lacunae "that deeply trouble me" as he said in his last epilogue and he has wanted to give this work, prepared with so much love and patience, the integrity possible in books of this kind.

Consequently, this edition is not a superficial retouching and update of the preceding book, but a substantial remake whose totality, including the documentary (amongst other things some aerial photographs have been added)can be useful not only to foreign visitors to Spain but also to any cultured Spaniard wishing to have the pleasure of knowing his country.

Consider, also, with what elegance Don José Páez Carrascosa transforms a simple informative fact and arouses interest and liking in the reader. One example well worth mentioning - In the introduction the author evokes, without saying it, the atmosphere of Greek drama, likening the area that surrounds Ronda to the Greek theatre of the IV century B.C. The reader, even he who is not able to comprehend the resemblance, will find himself transported to an unreal atmosphere in which, however, reality preserves its own life, which is the life of the spirit that nourishes from past to present and that understands the past in the immediacy of the present, awarding the subjet the impression of the soul, while it makes the soul suffer because of the imperfection of the subject.

And this miracle is renewed time after time during its exhibition in such a way that the reader and the visitor, without being aware of it, finds at the end that they have discovered, enclosed in the microcosms of Ronda, the ancient and modern qualities of Spain and they come to love this noble country.

Professor Michele Antonucci.

David Roberts. 1845

< New Bridge

*I*f we close our eyes and let our imagination carry us far away, from the highest peak we could see the town of Ronda, "The Veiled Beauty" as if born from the pregnant land, emerged from a dream.

The Theatre of Olympia on whose Proscenium the town was constructed and the Rondan actors have interpreted its prolonged history for 3.000 years. A platform or plateau at 750 mts. above sea level, formed by tertiary sediments of limestone and Miocene loam configurations wrapped and embraced by the stage of El Tajo, a precipice which is almost 500 mts. long with a maximum depth of 170 mts.

In the orchestra, called the Hoya de la Caldera (The Pit of the Cauldron) the Guadalevín (Wadi al-laban) River, lord and witness for such a long time, of our everyday lives in this theatre of our history. Its source is in the Sierra de Las Nieves and Oreganal, collecting on its way, near Ronda, the water from the streams of Toma, Arroyo Negro and the Culebras, and after leaving our town it joins the River Guadalcobacín to continue its course as the Guadiaro, where it flows near Gibraltar as the greatest river in all the Andalusian Mediterranean Basin.

Waters that caressed the sides of its bed, or that beat and lashed it in the raging winters and for centuries turned our mills of the gorge, irrigated our land and took with it more than one sorrow, at least one sigh and more than one wish.

Across the Proscenium, the majestic set of the Serranía of Ronda situated in the most western part of the Penibetic or Subbetic chain. To the northwest of this stage, the mountains of Los Merinos and Blanquilla formed by limestone and jurassic, which make way for the roads leading out to Burgo and to Campillos.

To the east the mountain ranges of Melequetín, Hidalga and Sierra de las Nieves where the highest point in the province of Málaga is found at 1.919 mts. La Torrecilla or Plazoletas, crossed by the road from San Pedro, Costa del Sol, which has become the main entrance to this great stage of the daily life of Ronda, through which a stream of visitors come and go daily.

To the south, the Sierra del Oreganal and Cartajima, calcareous masses that separate us from that great unknown Valley of Genal across whose foothills snakes the road to Algeciras and third entrance to this majestic stage.

The Hemicycle is formed on the southwest by a deep gulf, closed by the subbetic limestone of the Sierra de los Castillejos and Líbar where our River Guadiaro flows between narrow ravines. It continues and extends across the Sierras of San Cristóbal (1.640 mts.) and Grazalema which has one of the highest records of rainfall in Spain and is in the province of Cádiz. It drops to a depression that reaches the provinces of Cádiz and Seville, through which the River Guadalete snakes its way searching for its outlet in the crystalline waters of the Atlantic ocean, accompanied by the road that will bring us towards Seville-Jerez - Cádiz and the Valley of the Guadalquivir.

These obstacles of great hills and deep valleys have contributed to the isolation suffered by our town during centuries, to the refuge and protection for many during difficult periods of our history and they are loved and desired by all who know and visit it.

A geographical configuration, a mountainous and continental climate, despite its relative proximity to the sea, that have distinguished it, facing the depressions of its own environment and much more facing the Guadalquivir Valley, the Hoya of Málaga and the Campo de Gibraltar. An area of poor soil for agriculture, but with a great cattle raising area that constitutes the hydrographic basin of the two great rivers: the Guadalevin-Guadiaro whose source is in the Sierra de Las Nieves and the Guadalete in the Sierra de Grazalema. The former with its tributaries of the streams of Toma,

Ventilla and Sijuela being the means by which nature has managed to form this plateau or Proscenium.

Due to it being one of the areas with more rainfall in Andalusia, with an annual average of 700 mm. approximately, its vegetation is rich and complex as much in the scrubland as in the forest mass. Cork oak, carob trees, Aleppo pine and other species abound but what stands out above all others is the **Abies Pinsapo Boissier,** a plant from the Tertiary period. It is the most Meridional fir in Europe and the oldest species amongst all the firs around the Mediterranean; a botanical variety exclusive to this area although there are some examples in the Sierra de Gredos near Madrid. It is related to the fir from Rif in north Africa and very similar to the firs from Urales in Russia. Now we can have the pleasure of seeing this living fossil or relic of the world´s flora throughout our Serranía, Sierra de Las Nieves, Yunquera, Tolox or in the woods of Genalguacil and Casares and in the Reales of Sierra Bermeja, all in the province of Málaga; and also in the region of Sierra del Pinar between Grazalema and Benamahoma in the province of Cádiz.

Really we have to admit that in this great theatre or circus of Gods that forms our Serranía, Mother Nature has been very generous and although mankind has left its mark after thousands of years of habitat and its architectural-monumental complex may be one of the most beautiful and best preserved throughout Europe, the sensation due to its location, its orography, its light and colour convert it into a dream of a town, an unrealizable sigh, a prodigy of the divine, into a place to dream and discover "La Bella Tapada" (The Veiled Beauty); "La Hermosa Desconocida"(The Beautiful Stranger).

Old Ramparts

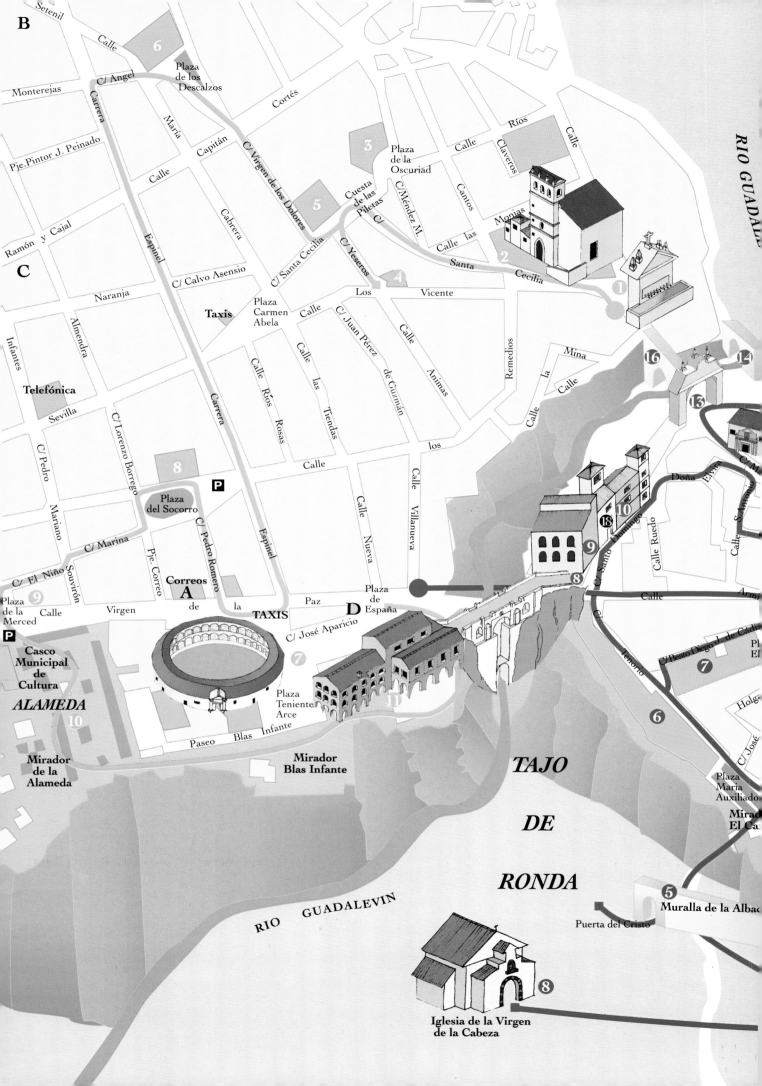

B

Setenil

Calle

6

Montereras

C/ Angel

Plaza
de los
Descalzos

Carrera

Pje.Pintor J. Peinado

Maria

Capitán

Calle

Cortés

3

C/ Virgen de los Dolores

Plaza
de la
Oscuriad

Calle

Ríos

Claveros

Calle

Cabrera

5

Cuesta
de las
Piletas

C/Méndez M.

Monjas

Calle

C

Ramón y Cajal

Calle

C/ Calvo Asensio

C/ Santa Cecilia

C/ Yeseros

Cantos

Calle las

2

Espinel

Naranja

Taxis

Plaza
Carmen
Abela

4

Los

Vicente

Santa

Cecilia

1

Infantes

Almendra

Calle

Calle

C/ Juan Pérez de Guzmán

Calle Animas

Remedios

Mina

Calle

16

14

Telefónica

Sevilla

C/ Lorenzo Borrego

Calle Ríos

Rosas

Calle las Tiendas

la

Calle

13

C/ Pedro

8

Calle

los

Calle

C/ Anto

Mariano

P

Plaza
del Socorro

Espinel

Calle Nueva

Calle Villanueva

9

Doña Elvira

10

18

C/ Marina

C/ Pedro Romero

C/ El Niño Souvirón

Pje. Correo

**Correos
A**

de la

Paz

TAXIS

Plaza
de
España

D

8

C/ Santo Domingo

Calle Ruedo

9

Plaza
de la
Merced

Calle

Virgen

C/ José Aparicio

Calle

C/ Beato Diego J. de Cádiz

7

P

**Casco
Municipal
de
Cultura**

7

Plaza
Teniente
Arce

11

Jenorio

6

Holga

C/ José

ALAMEDA

10

Paseo Blas Infante

**Mirador
de la
Alameda**

**Mirador
Blas Infante**

TAJO

Plaza
Maria
Auxiliador

Mirad
El Ca

DE

5

RONDA

Muralla de la Alba

Puerta del Cristo

RIO GUADALEVIN

8

**Iglesia de la Virgen
de la Cabeza**

RIO GUADALE

ONUMENTS

RY 1

Church of our Lady of the Incarnation
City Hall
Convent of St. Isabel of the Angels
Mondragón Palace
Ramparts of the Albacara
House of Saint John Bosco
Church of Our Lady of Peace
The New Bridge
Convent of Santo Domingo
10 House of the Moorish King
11 Minaret of Saint Sebastian
12 Palace of the Marquis of Salvatierra
13 Gate of Philip V
14 Old Bridge or Arabian Bridge
15 Arab Baths
16 Bridge of San Miguel
17 Ramparts of Xijara
18 Museum-Palace of Santa Pola

ITINERARY 2

1 Fountain of Eight Spouts
2 Parish of Padre Jesús
3 Mozarabic Church of La Oscuridad
4 Inn of Our Lady of Souls
5 Chapel of Our Lady of Sorrows
6 Church of Los Descalzos
7 Bullring
8 Church of Socorro
9 Convent of La Merced
10 Alameda- Promenade of the Gorge
11 Parador

ITINERARY 3

1 The Holy Spirit Church
2 Ramparts of Almocábar
3 Gate of Almocábar
4 Gate of Charles V
5 Church of Our Lady of Grace
6 Convent of the Franciscans
7 Convent of San Francisco
8 Rupestrian Church of Virgen de la Cabeza

A- Post Office **B- Bus Terminal** **C- Rail Road Station** **D- Tourist Office**

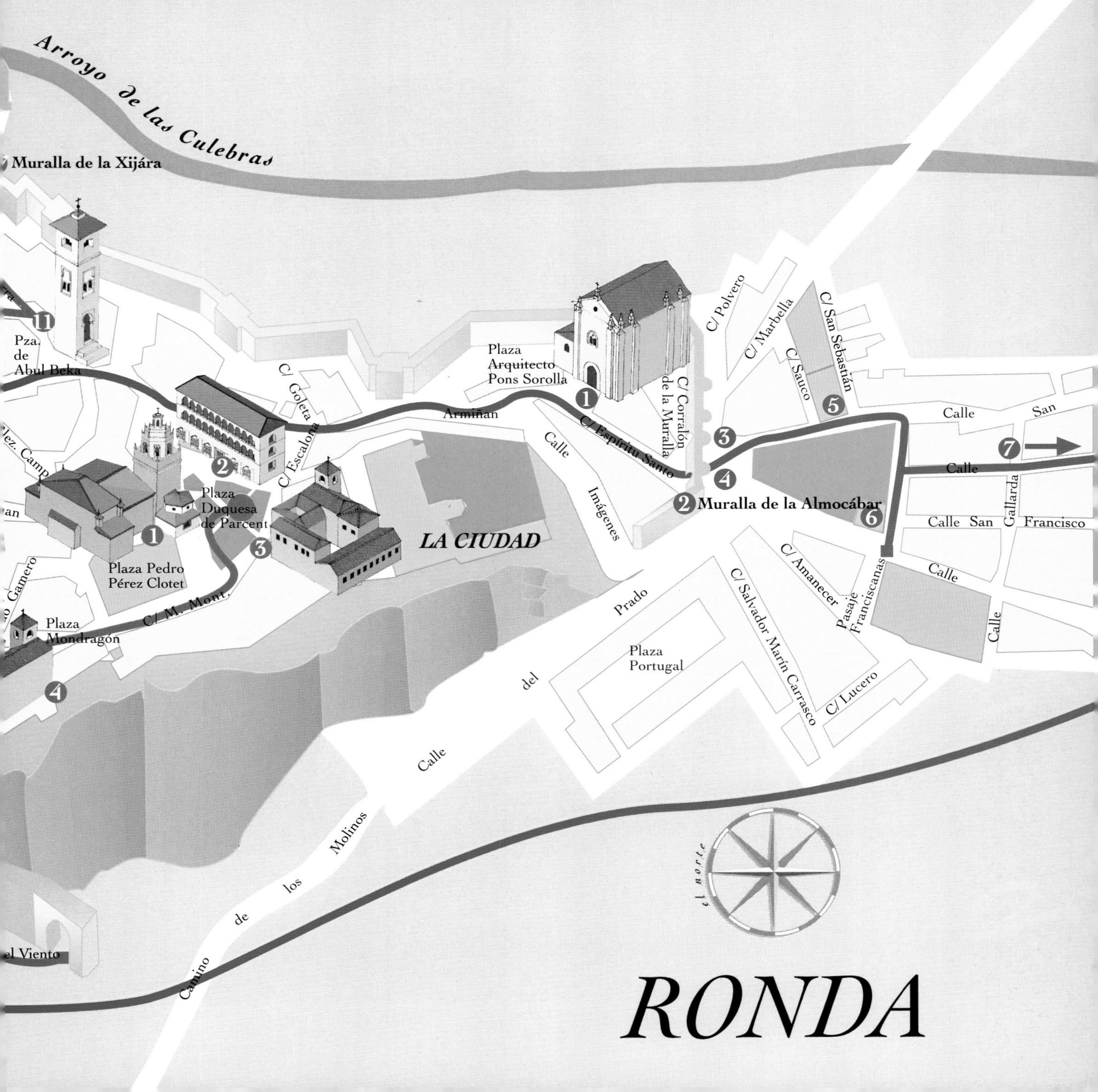
Arroyo de las Culebras
Muralla de la Xijára
Pza. de Abul Beka
C/ Goleta
C/ Escalona
Plaza Duquesa de Parcent
Plaza Pedro Pérez Clotet
C/ M. Mont.
Plaza Mondragón
Arminan
Plaza Arquitecto Pons Sorolla
Calle Imágenes
C/ Espíritu Santo
C/ Corralón de la Muralla
C/ Polvero
C/ Marbella
C/ Sauco
C/ San Sebastián
LA CIUDAD
Muralla de la Almocábar
Calle San
Calle
Calle San Francisco
Gallarda
C/ Amanecer
Pasaje Franciscanas
C/ Salvador Marín Carrasco
C/ Lucero
Plaza Portugal
Calle del Prado
Camino de los Molinos
el Viento
el norte
RONDA

<Gate of the Xijara
Wood engraving by David Bomberg

Primitive man looked for simplicity in order to develop his way of life: security and shelter in the sheer, craggy peaks; an abundance of grazing land, water, woods and the possibilities for hunting and mining. These were characteristics of our mountain range and the initial reasons why Prehistoric man settled in our region.

We have knowledge of human presence in our region (the Valleys of Genal and Guadiaro) since the mid Palaeolithic period .The cave of La Pileta, Benaoján being a prehistoric collection of rupestrian art, human remains, ceramics and lithographs.These are of outstanding interest in the World´s Prehistory as they cover the superior Palaeolithic period up to the Neolithic period.

At the same time the numerous remains of the incidental megalithic monuments in the Rondan plateau such as: Los Arenosos, Cortijo Del Chopo, El Gigante, Encinas Borrachas and others corroborate continual settlements in our region. Recent excavations, in situ, of the old quarters of the town where remains of ceramics, pots of different sizes and bowls, little blades and chips of silex or flint, small polished axes, needles made from bone... with many megalithic elements, such as polished stones (hand operated mills, hammers, axes) gallery dolmens, a rudimentary furnace for smelting minerals, ceramics of campanulate form...or the very important mould for casting bronze swords of Sa Idda (from VIIth. century B.C.) prove the existence of continuous settlements in the old quarters from Neolithic period to date.

The historic origins of the city of Ronda go back to **the Bastulo Celts** who called it Arunda. According to Pliny, the Celts established in Celtic Baeturia reached our mountains in the VIth. century B.C. and according to Iforo, the Celts dominated our regions mixing with the Iberian population and all these Megalithic settlements were taken over and controlled by them. It would appear that this was an advanced and isolated Celtic domain, in contact with the Tartessian civilization, although from the year 500 B.C. the Celts appear to have occupied all the boundaries of these Andalusian regions.

Ronda had very little commercial dealings with the Phoenicians because when they came to this part of the world they found, close to Arunda, a little hamlet, which had been founded by the Iberians and was called Acinipo, where they settled and improved its constructions. It was an ideal situation considering their commercial aspirations with the interior of the country as Acinipo was half way between

Bulls Eyes. Typical Grill

Málaga and Cádiz which were also Phoenician colonies.

The Greeks sailed towards the Western Mediterranean where they began audacious competition with the Phoenicians, but avoided the Punic domains of the Straits. They skirted our mountain range searching for an interior route in order to trade with the Tartessians and also for the flow of the Tagus river, in this periplus Arunda becomes a Greek contact base under the name of Runda, but their influence disappears with the fall of Phocaeans after the battle of Alalia (535 B.C.).

During the predominance of **Carthage**, our indigenous towns nourished the Carthaginian armies for almost three centuries during their battles against Greeks and Romans.

As a result of the Second Punic War **the Romans** fought in Hispania against the Carthaginians and the Roman Chief Lucius Marcus, legate of Publius Cornelius Scipio, carried out military operations throughout our region and the Straits area before taking Gaddir (206 B.C.). With the Carthaginians expelled, the Romans begin to take control of the inland tribes. Their political administrative system brings serious changes to our mountain range and to our town, and in the year 197 B.C., they begin to manage and organise their hispanic ruling in two provinces: Citerior and Ulterior with Tarraco (Tarragona) and Corduba (Córdoba) as their respective capitals. For a long time our district of Arunda fluctuated between these two provinces until the division of Augustus it finally became a part of the province of Hispania Ulterior Baetica and under the administration of the Sevillian Convento according to some and under the Astigitano according to Pliny.

Arunda was one of the 29 cities of the Betica region that enjoyed the old rights of Latium. Acinipo (land of the wines) had the same good fortune but thanks to its geographical position it became a big city, becoming a municipality with power to mint coins and later its inhabitants had the same rights as any citizen from Imperial Rome.

Although it is certain that the Roman archaeological remains, materials and inscriptions found to date - tegulae, tombs, memorial stones, silos, acquaducts, statues, amphorae...are not of great importance it is also true that both Acinipo and Arunda were involved in the historical events that were to change and favour our land.

After the betrayal of the praetor Galba and the following rebellion of Viriato, at the head of his Lusitanian and Celtic villages fighting for independence, Arunda and Acinipo were to be witness and participants of the raids and incursions of these people during the almost 20 years of implacable bat-

Arrival of ladies in old fashion to the bullring

Hanging Houses

tles against Rome. (War of Fire, according to Polybus).

The death of the Lusitanian chief in 139 B.C. and the pacification of the Celtiberian villages gave way, after the Roman victory, to the creation of strategic points as defensive centres and so in the year 132 B.C. General Scipio Eamilianus founded an equestrian order in Arunda - Legio Arundesis - and ordered the construction of the castle of Laurus, whose objectives were obvious: the appeasement and control of the Celtiberian tribes, always close to rebellion, and for the desire for freedom.

From the end of the IInd. century B.C. to the end of the Ist. century B.C. the Empire would be witness to the squabbles of its leading men supporting political parties. In these civil wars the Spaniards were to be a decisive factor.

Their favours were to be disputed by Sulla, Sertorius and Pompey and later by Caesar and Octavius, reflecting clearly the intrinsic importance of this period for Spanish history and in the structure of the Empire. In these lars, Sertorius, at war against Pompey, destroyed the city of Arunda and in the year 45 B.C. a temple was constructed in our city to commemorate the victory of Caius Caesar over Gnaeus and Sextus, sons of Pompey.

Once Spain is pacified, with the unification of language, commerce, development of roads and public works, it becomes the second most important country in the Empire. The domination passes in our country with

the assimilation of its culture and customs by the natives but they maintain their natural position and privileged situation next to the cross-roads of the Roman roads coming from Cádiz (via Zahara) and from Gibraltar (via the valley of Guadiaro) towards El Burgo and Iluro.

With the invasion of **the Sueves, the Vandals, the Alans** and later the Visigoths, both Arunda and Acinipo were destroyed and pillaged. One act that stands out in this period is the help requested by the Gothic King,

Gate of Almocábar

Atanagildo from Justinian, Emperor of the Byzantines, in his battle against Agila. Justinian is rewarded with the south-east coast of Spain and creates in this part of the Mediterranean, the province of Orospeda, which includes Ronda.

The Greek Byzantines search in our land for the place which was for their ancestors, Runda. They discover the ruins of Acinipo and Runda, and finding the former in better conditions, and also they preferred its location, they settled in it and called it Runda; the town was to be recuperated once again by the Visigoths in the time of Suintila but they eventually abandoned it, leaving it completely demolished and so the area became rural. This is why, by tradition, the missing town of Acinipo is called "Old Ronda".

With the decline of Acinipo, our Roman-Visigothic Arunda continues to be a stronghold and defence for our coast against the dangerous Berbers.

In the year 711, **Tariq Ben Ziyad** lands in Gibraltar and Algeciras, leading his troops to defeat the Visigoth King, Don Rodrigo, in the battle of Guadalete, or according to other authors in the Laguna of La Janda, immediately continuing to Ecija, Córdoba and Toledo.

General Musa Ben-Nusayr arrives in Spain in the year 712 and instead of joining forces with his lieutenant Tariq, he prefers to take possession of the towns not already conquered by him, such as Medina Sidonia, Seville, Carmona or Ronda and so Abd al-Aziz, Musa´s son, conquers our town and its castle Laurel in the year 713. He immediately orders the construction of a new town on top of its ruins which is to be called Izna-Rand-Onda, the town of the castle. It becomes,immediately, a great point of communication

JoséRuiz, popular Rondan

and union between the future Emirate of Córdoba and the African territories.

It is obvious that Izna-Rand-Onda was recognised as being important to the new conquerors and in its administrative organisation they convert it into the capital of Tacoronna, one of the five coras or regions in which the south of Andalusia was divided under the province of Seville. It included all the land of these mountains and thus from a simple castle it became a great town.

During the first years of Muslim domination the population of Ronda and its Serrania (or mountain range) was practically all African, Berber tribes coming from the Atlas mountains merged with an autochthonous population of Greek-Roman, Gothic and Hebrew origin. According to the historian Ibn Hazm "To the region of Ronda and the Valley of Genal came the Walhasa, tribes from the mountains of North Africa, with a minority of Arab families".

This ethnic origin of our population was the cause of multiple rebellions against the Emirate of Córdoba; that of Umar-Ibn-Hafsún standing out above all others.

He was born in 854, near our town in the hamlet of Torricella, near the castle of Ibn Auta, Parauta, in the heart of the Valley of Genal. He was of noble Gothic-Christian origin and he managed to unite the unrest of the Muslims and Christians against the abuses of the Arab nobility. At the head of a great army he roused them to rebel against the power of the Umayyads, keeping them in check during the period 899-917.

He situated his headquarters in the Fort of Bobastro between the valley of Abdalagis, Ardales and Alora in the province of Málaga. The bravery and fame of this highlander spread more and more as it became aware that every day numerous voluntaries, searching

A pleasant spot

for freedom and independence, joined his armies. He controlled all of the pronvince of Málaga and part of Cádiz, including Algeciras. The provinces of Granada and Jaén took orders from him and he advanced as well through the province of Cordoba, conquering the town of Cabra. He even thought of naming himself Emir of Spain for which he began negotiations with the Caliph Abbasid.

Abd-Al-Rahman III tried to defeat him without success as Umar had meanwhile died, invincible, in his fortress of Bobastro in the year 917. The descendants of Umar-Ibn-Hafsún continued the war during the next ten years and were finally defeated by the Caliph of Cordoba, who destroyed all his work. Umar-Ibn-Hafsún is to be praised for his efforts to win independence for our region. He could have achieved his wishes had he not embraced the Christian faith and in doing so, alienate his Muslim followers.

On the death of Almansor, (Al-Mansur, Victor by the Grace of God) the Civil War destroyed the unfortunate Kingdom of Hixen II with partisan and ethnic differences and confrontations, causing the fall of the Western Umayyad Caliphate and the introduction of approximately 30 small kingdoms (or taifas).

In the years 1014-1016 a Berber lieutenant of Almansor takes advantage of the breakdown of the Córdoba caliphate and creates the Kingdom of the Banu Ifrán of Ronda, whose area covers the old region of Tacoronna.

Abú-Nur governs in peace and prosperity for 40 years, what was called from that period onwards, Madinat Runda. He founds new villages in the mountain range and improves and constructs important buildings such as mosques, palaces and baths. He reinforces ramparts and defences, opening a main entrance in the southern part, The Gate of Almocábar, and another on the eastern end, The Gate of Xijara, communicating the old suburbs with the Madinat.

The independence of Ronda didn´t last long. It was coveted as much by the kings of Málaga as by those of Seville. Abú Nur was not free from the greed of the Sevillian King al-Muthadid who plotted a conspiracy to wipe out the petty Kings of the three adjoining Berber occupations: Ronda, Arcos and Morón but Abú Nur had already died and his son Abú Nasar was assassinated by al-Muthadid, and his kingdom was then incorporated into that of Seville in 1066. The poet King al-Muthadid sang to what he considered the jewel in his crown "The best fortified, you are the best gem in my kingdom. Oh, Ronda mine!"

As a consequence of the break-up of the Andalusian unity and of the Christian threats, especially Castilian and Aragonese, the petty kings reacted by calling the Almorávids (warriors of the tribes from Atlas) to their aid. Taking advantage of the general discontent and the religious laxity of the Andalusian population all the petty kingdoms of Al-Andalus are conquered and Madinat Ronda is annexed in 1091.

The Empire of the Almorávids is short-lived as they are accused by the Almohads (fighters of the faith) of immoral administration and disturbances or unrest and they are expelled from Morocco and Al- Andalus. In 1146 the Almohads enter the Peninsula and by 1192 are ruling practically all Muslim Spain, but are defeated by the Christians in the battle of Navas de Tolosa in the year 1212. Thus the danger that these Berber invasions represented disappears with the advance of the Christian Reconquest.

Starting with this great Christian victory the reconquest was established in Al-Andalus. Fernando III conquers Ubeda in 1233, Córdoba in 1236 and Seville in 1248. Due to these events the petty king of Jaén, Muhammad Ibn al-Alhamar (son of the Red) decides to transfer his court to Granada in 1238, and founds the

Popular architecture

Ladies in goyesca fashion

Ronda House. Hall

Ronda Sings

Nasrid Kingdom. Here he has protection from the Penibetica mountain range, and so his authority spreads throughout the actual provinces of Almería, Granada and Málaga.

His son Muhammad II, forgotten and afraid of the reinforcement of the power of Castille, approaches the Emir Abu Yusuf Yaqub in Fez, founder of the Banu Marin Empire. The Banu Marins cross to the peninsula and settle in the towns of Tarifa, Algeciras and Ronda in 1275, using these fortified towns as bases in order to raid the Guadalquivir Valley. This, in turn, gave a certain tranquillity to Granada, the last Islamic stronghold in Andalusia.

In 1295 the Banu Marins return to Morocco and give up their fortified towns of Andalucía, which are taken over by the Nasrid King Muhammad III; one of these towns being Madinat Ronda. However a Rondan family of

San Francisco Convent. Façade >

Ronda from the Church Virgen de la Cabeza

the Banu al-Hakim opposes the agreement and declares himself independent.

Chronicles of the Kings of Castille tell us that in this period "The Moors of Ronda were the most brave and bold of this country". Ronda and its mountains become very important at this time of the history of the Reconquest. Its position as an impregnable fortress between the borders of the Christian Kingdoms of the Guadalquivir valley, the Kingdoms of Granada and the north of Africa with which they had great ethnic and cultural ties, puts it in a situation of being able to change from allies to enemies with great ease, being fought over by both Granada and by the Christians of Lower Andalusia, and especially from the **XIII C.** when the Straits of Gibraltar became a problem of survival for everyone.

Alfonso XI relates how he destroyed land and vineyards in Ronda, Antequera and Archidona hoping to weaken his enemies due to lack of food. According to chronicles, the Castillian King arrived in Ronda as far as the Mercadillo area where he fought in a campaign that lasted four days, but through lack of provisions he was obliged to abandon the battle.

In the year 1314, the King of Granada, Ismail I frightened by the advance of the Christian forces, once again asks the Banu Marins for help. The Emperor Yusuf Abú Ya´qub gives assistance and as a

reward is given the towns of Ronda, Algeciras and Marbella.

As a consequence of the advance of King Alfonso XI, following the conquest of Olvera in 1327, and Cañete and Ortexícar in 1330, the Emperor of Fez sends his son Abomelik at the front of a large army, whose principal feat was to be the conquest of Gibraltar in 1333.

Abomelik installed his court in Ronda, and in doing so, this period increased in prosperity and splendour as he constructed important buildings such as the Bridge, the Alhama in the old outskirts, the staircase of La Mina (the mine) with 360 steps made straight from the bare rock so that water could be provided to the whole town in case of attack. Oil and flour mills were built in the bottom of the gorge which would supply the entire local population.

However, this Rondan king ruled for a very short time as he encountered the troops of Alfonso XI in 1338 near the town of Jerez de la Frontera and was killed by a christian soldier. Finally, after his defeat in the battle of Salado, near Tarifa, the 28th. of October 1340, the Sultan of Fez, Abul-Hassan, returns for good to his African territories and with the Conquest of Algeciras by King Alfonso XI in the year 1344, the domination of the Banu Marins in Andalusia was finally over.

Pinsapo in Bloom

From that moment on, the subjection of the Kingdom of Granada to Castille is reaffirmed and our town Madinat Ronda finds itself involved in the games of alliance within the Nasrid Kingdom.

During the **XVth.** century, Ronda weakens due to the furious attacks by the Christians, and the threat becomes serious when, in 1407, after the Conquest of the village of Zahara, the young Prince, Don Fernando of Antequera makes his way to Ronda and surrounds it, arriving at the Mercadillo at the front of his troops "But it was too strong and well guarded with many defending it and winter was approaching".

Pedro Romero celebrations. September

The conquest of the city of Ronda was not possible until the Catholic Monarchs came to the throne of Aragon and Castille, solving the problem of the civil war in Castille and the confrontation with Portugal.

Finally they decide to finish for once and for all with the last bastion of the Arab domination in Spain and to unify all the Kingdoms of the Peninsula. They meticulously prepare, from a military angle as well as diplomatically, the conquest of the Nasrid Kingdom, taking into consideration how important it is, and how it had an ever-increasing population of Moors who were seeking refuge from a Christian attack; so Fernando the Catholic King conquers the Algarbe of Málaga, to the west of the province during the campaign of 1485, and follows with the entrance into Ronda on the 22nd of May in the same year.

The reconquest of Zahara by the Muslims of Ronda at the end of December 1481 and the loss of its garrison, was what brought about the beginning of the conquest of the Kingdom of Granada. Head of a natural region, and solid stronghold, right on the Christian border it naturally produced anxiety and brought on Christian revenge by taking the city of Alhama, residence of the Sultan, close to the city of Granada itself.

Zahara is recuperated in October 1483 and the Monarchs transfer to Córdoba where they begin to create a modern army and stock up on weapons.

Following a plan to siege the towns and make sudden attacks, Alora is taken on 20th. of June 1484 and following that, Alozaina, continuing with the capture of the small town of Setenil, in the actual province of Cádiz. On the 15th. of April 1485 the King leaves Córdoba and marches towards Puente Genil and four days later has already taken positions in Cártama, Coín and Benamaqués.

Hamet El Zegrí, Governor of Ronda and chief of the tribe named after him leaves the city in order to defend the towns attacked by Fernando the Catholic King. Despite his bravery and efforts, Coín is defeated on the 27th. of April and the following day the same fate falls on Cártama.

With the entire valley of Cártama conquered, the Christian troops reach the actual gates of the city of Málaga, where Hamet El Zegrí manages to arrive with reinforcements and eventually saves it.

Coat of Arms

May 5th., the Marquis of Cádiz aims for the conquest of the city of Ronda, accompanied by Don Pedro Enrique with 3,000 horses and 8,000 soldiers on foot, having been previously informed by Yusuf Xarif, one of the important men of the town, that (according to the author Valera) "The city was almost depopulated and badly defended and that he would show them a sure route by which they could easily take over the city, trusting that the King and Queen would show him mercy".

King Fernando makes his way towards Antequera and Archidona, laying siege to the town of Loja in order to distract the troops of Málaga. At the same time he sends artillery through Cártama

and Coín, towards Teba where he was to meet up with all the troops for the conquest of the city of Ronda of which the Marquis of Cádiz was to take up position as governor.

On the 11th. of May 1485, Hamet El Zegri, Governor of Ronda is informed that the real intention of the Christian army was not to conquer Ronda, but while feigning attacks against the towns of Ronda and Loja in order to distract his troops, a second Christian army was on its way to the final conquest of the city of Málaga, which obviously was not well protected.

The next day,12th. of May, Hamet El Zegrí sees how the Christian troops set up camp near Ronda, and meanwhile has no doubt about the information brought to him. He prepares his army and marches to defend Málaga, naming in his absence Abraham al Háquim as governor.

The following day King Fernando orders a siege on the town of Ronda; his army making a total of 9,000 horses and 20,000 soldiers on foot, with 4.000 horses and 5.000 infantry bringing up the rear in case of necessity

Hamet El Zegrí, on route to Málaga, hears of the siege of Ronda and becomes furious; deciding to return with all his troops he tries to destroy the Christian soldiers bringing up the rear but all his efforts were useless.

The circle closed around the city and on the 14th an attack against it is decided. One of the most decisive factors which brought about the accelerated fall of the city was, apart from the betrayal, the tremendous use of artillery

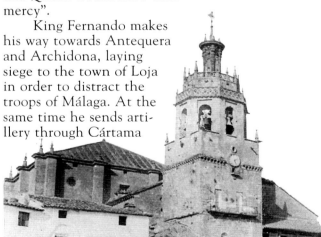

Square of Santa María. At the beginning of the XXth. (Foto Miguel Martín)

Religious detail. Palace of Salvatierra

which was distributed in three points: the first was pointed at the octagonal tower of the castle; the second to the lower walls of the gate of Almocábar and the third was in the east end, at the level of Los Tejares dominating the whole city.

It is worth noting that in the conquest of Ronda, lombards were used as a bellicose artillery device that hurled out lumps of pitch and sulphur and destroyed all the buildings they hit, causing great confusion and fear amongst the people.

After seven days of fierce battles, and without water supply, as it had been cut off by the Marquis of Cádiz, according to the historian Valera. "Friday the 13th. they fought over the mine which was bravely defended by the Moors. It resulted in many injured and some deaths, but despite everything it was taken over, and a tower in the river from where the Moors got their

water, was destroyed ...; a breach was opened in the eight sided tower and later it toppled over". "The artillery fired so many continuous discharges that the Moors who were controlling the Cidba could hardly hear each other, they had nowhere to sleep and knew not where to get help, because the lombards where knocking down walls and houses", according to Hernando del Pulgar.

In the midst of the fighting, the second lieutenant Alonso Yáñez Fajardo with his sword in one hand and the banner of the cross in the other, after many efforts, manages to place the banner on top of the ruins of the tower. This gave more determination to the Christian troops in their fight, demoralising the Moors who flee for refuge in the fortress. The Governor, on seeing the desperate situation, hoists the white flag, surrendering the city.

This is seen by Hamet El Zegrí, who for ten days tried desperately to break the siege, blind with rage, returns with his men to Málaga in whose defence he dies in 1487 but not before cursing the defenders of the city of Ronda, accusing them of being traitors and crying for the loss of his beloved city, Flower of the Kingdom of Granada. *"Shame, shame, on those who have betrayed their brothers and dishonoured their homeland! Oh, my Ronda! Oh, how unhappy I am! Why was I so gullible as to leave through the Gate of Almocábar?".*

King Fernando agrees to hold a parley, and orders all hostilities to cease, granting to the defeated their life and all their worldly goods.

The majority of the Muslim population went to the mountain villages under Christian rule. Others went to Africa and those important men who had made the pact or prepared the surrendering of the city went to live in the province of Seville, in the town of Alcalá de Guadaira to be precise, where they were given homes and properties that had belonged to Judaizers condemned by the Inquisition.

Out of the dungeons and jails came the Christian prisoners, half dead and emaciated. The majority of them had been made prisoners in the battle of Axarquia, with a total of approximately 400, forty of them being women. They were given food and clothing and were taken to Cordoba to be received by Queen Isabel. Afterwards they were sent to places of their own choice. To commemorate this event Queen Isabel ordered the chains with which they were made prisoners, to be hung outside the church of San Juan de los Reyes in Toledo.

The fall of Ronda was what decided the whole of the Algarbe of Málaga; all the towns of the area resorted to surrender with the exception

Aerial view of Ronda >

Carving in Ronda. House of San Juan Bosco

of the districts of Casarabonela and Marbella, which came later.

With the banners of the Catholic Church, those of the Crusades and the King of Castile placed in the Tower of Homenaje (or Homage) of the Castle, King Fernando V of Aragon entered into the city of Ronda with great triumph, on the 24th. of May. The old main mosque was converted and consecrated to the Christian faith under the advocation of Our Lady of the Incarnation, to whom Queen Isabel had great devotion, solemn Te Deum was sung there, and the King, turning towards the ruins of the octagonal tower ordered the construction of a church in the same place, under the advocation of the

Paco "The Farrier"

Holy Spirit as the conquest of Ronda had coincided with Pentecost of that year .

The King, anxious to be reunited with the Queen who waited impatiently in Córdoba, arrived at the city triumphantly, leaving the Count of Ribadeo, Don Pedro de Villandrado behind as Governor of the city.

After the conquest of Ronda, a parcelling out of lands was made between noblemen and knights that had taken part in the Conquest of the city. Juan Torres and the lawyer Juan de la Fuente were sent to Ronda and Marbella, and other villages, valleys and land taken from the Moors so that they could share out the houses and properties amongst the Christian inhabitants who had once again gone to settle there.

And so, dated 25th. of July 1485 by Royal Warrant the Monarchs declare "It is our wish that, in order to govern well this very noble city of Ronda, won by us from the Moors, it should have 13 Councillors for life: Antonio de Fonseca - Governor, Commander and Supreme Magistrate of the city; Ruy López de Toledo - Treasurer of the King and Queen and Juan de la Fuente, Juan de Merlo, Pedro del Castillo, Juan Dávila, Mateo Luzón, Juan de Villalba, Alonso Yáñez Fajardo, Lope de Cárdenas, Pedro Lado, Hernando de Zafra and Gonzalo de Guzmán to be its lawyers. The city was divided into 5 districts or parishes with the names of its churches; Our Lady of the Incarnation, Holy Spirit, Santiago, St. John the Baptist and St. Sebastian. There were to be 12 Jurymen, a second lieutenant, a notary, 6 perpetual clerks, a Mayor of the town council, a constable and 2 mayors. The areas of Burgo, Montecorto and all the other villages and places that used to belong to the town were to come under the jurisdiction of Ronda. The laws for the Government and Town Council were to be the same as those given to Seville by

Mondragón Palace. Façade >

King Fernando III. The coat of arms of the city would display the following: *"A golden yoke with silver tethers and a bunch of silver arrows on a red field"*. No Jews could live in Ronda, nor spend more than three days there, "with the exception of Israel, our translator of Arabic."

They continue in the same way, parcelling out the land between churches, monasteries and hospitals and order the construction of monasteries in the area where the camps of Marquis of Cádiz, the Count of Benavente and the Master of Alcántara are situated; they give land to the Royal Hospital and have the Hermitage of the Assumption built. Inmediately a record is made of the private people and noblemen to whom the land has been given, Alonso Yáñez Fajardo, the hero of the conquest of Ronda being the most favoured. Bricklayers and carpenters are brought from Seville to complete the restoration of the fort, walls and gates of the city, and the balls and projectiles fired by the lombards during the attack are placed outside the entrance walls in the form of crucifixes in memory of such a great victory.

Ronda was an estate, granted for the upkeep of the Royal house of Prince Juan to whom the Parliament of Toledo swore their allegiance in 1480, as Prince of Asturias. The future heir to the thrown married Margaret of Austria in Burgos, on the 19th. of March 1497. On his death she took over possession of the estate of our city. In 1499 Princess Margaret goes to Flanders to become Governor and returns all her dominions to the Royal Family of Spain.

Already irregularities were starting to be seen in the administration of the city, increasing considerably the sales tax imposed on the products that arrived to our city to feed it. Under these circumstances the suppliers decided to stay outside the gates, forming centres of population or markets, that were the origin of the actual districts of Mercadillo and San Francisco. In time, the district of San Francisco was to become the agricultural quarter and the Mercadillo the service area which developed so

Popular architecture

much that it eventually occupied all the northern area of the Tajo.

In the mountains of Granada, the Moriscos (those Moors who had not accepted Christianity during the Reconquest) were rebelling due to the fact that the agreements made after the conquest between King Boabdil and King Fernando were not being carried out. Because of this the Moorish population of Ronda and its mountains sent to ask for security before the obligatory conversions.Queen Isabel replied "You have my Royal word of honour that neither the King nor I shall allow that any of your wives, children or grandchildren, shall be made Christian by force, against your wishes". Her reply arrived late. The Moors were convinced that the wishes of the King and Queen would be that they should embrace Christianity and meanwhile decided to join the

Holm oaks at dusk. Setenil mountains

Moriscos from the Alpujarras,(mountains of Granada).

The blaze of the uprising began in January 1501 and by the end of February of the same year the Earl of Cifuentes had arrived in Ronda with 300 horses and 2.000 men, together with the Earl of Ureña and Alfonso de Aguilar. On the 22nd. of February the people of Montejaque and Benaoján with the arrival of the Castillian sodiers, accepted Christianity.The campaign of the Earl of Cifuentes lasted one month and finished tragically, as on the 18 March, Alfonso de Aguilar, brother of the Gran Capitán, Francisco Rodrigo de Madrid and Pedro de Córdoba, were attacked and lost their lives in the cliffs of Monarda in the Bermeja range. Before such a state of affairs and the news of a defeat, King Fernando transferred to Ronda at the end of March in order to reinforce and personally control such a serious situation on his own scene.

After certain agreements the Moors involved in the rebellion were allowed to go to Africa and abandon the mountain range or take the road to conversion and return to their home and belongings. King Fernando returned to Granada the7th. of May.

With the appeasement of the mountain range and the long period of 40 years that the Emperor Charles V gave to the Moriscos to abandon their style of dress and customs, the Moors of Ronda developed a great commercial and artisan work, but saw themselves tarnished by an attempted uprising, the burning of archives in 1538, or continuous contact with Turks and Berbers until finally the rebellion in Sierra Bermeja and the Valley of Genal between 1568 and 1570 brought about the arrival of the Duke of Arcos to the city of Ronda. Once the uprising was under control, the Moriscos were sent to the regions of Extremadura and Galicia by order of King Felipe II which gave way to an economic decline in the area that was to become worse when they were all finally expelled in the year 1609, by order of King Felipe III.

Important events continue to form our history and after the uprising of the Castillian communities, representatives from the most important towns of Andalusia: Seville, Córdoba, Ecija, Jérez, Antequera, Cádiz, Ronda, Andujar, Carmona, Torredonjimeno, Arjona and Porcuna, meet in La Rambla, in the province of Córdoba in January 1521 to decide on the position of each one, facing the local uprisings Ronda remained faithful to Charles I.

The results of that meeting on the 17th. of January 1521, were passed to the King by the

Procurator of Ronda, Luis Méndez Sotomayor, who on hearing of the loyalty of our town to himself exclaimed *"Oh Ronda, strong and faithful"* which is the motto that appears as a border on the coat of arms granted to us by the Catholic Kings and that the Emperor himself ratified by letter dated the 16th. September of the same year. In 1547 the Emperor added two columns of Hercules to his coat of arms and the Latin motto "Non Plus Ultra" later deleting the "Non". As a result of this, Ronda followed his example, and the coat of arms of our city took shape and has remained this way ever since.

The **XVI and XVII** centuries were those that gave our beloved Ronda its actual structure just as we know it today. The main part - Madinat- starts to be known as "The City"; the higher district until today as the Holy Spirit district, and the Bajo or lower part, abandoned by the majority of its neighbours, with the installation of industry, tanneries and brothels. It was to be called from then until today District of San Miguel under the advocation of the Holy Cross.

The new districts of the Mercadillo and San Francisco were to be symbols of a new development and a new society. Saint Christopher is chosen as patron saint; Comercio becomes the

Door and tiles. Casa del Rey Moro

The Beautiful Stranger

main street,(Long street or Armiñán street as it is known today) churches, convents, hospices, hospitals in the town, and shops, inns and taverns in the Mercadillo were built. Our people from Ronda go and help in the many deeds of the Empire; always prepared to answer the Royal call.

But the **XVIII** century was the one which projected our city towards the future, leaving behind the concern for its own defence. It became as rich in livestock as in industry and mining.Commerce flourished and the population grew tremendously which gave way to the construction of very symbolic buildings for our city, e.g. The Bull Ring, The New Bridge, The Gate of Felipe V, etc.

The social and urbanistic development of the town was affected with the arrival of the French on the10th. of February 1810, with José Bonaparte himself at the front. He stayed in the house of the Marquis of Moctezuma, which is today the Santa Teresa school.

It is true that the French arrived without great opposition but we should not forget the contribution of Ronda with 1.400 veterans for the armies of the Regions of Seville and Granada led by General Castaño, which defeated General Dupont in Bailen the 22nd. of July 1808.This caused the immediate disappearance of a whole army and the first defeat suffered by Napoleon`s troops in open country which obliged the King José Bonaparte to leave Madrid and the Emperor himself then took command of all his armies in Spain.

From then on all the resistance against the French concentrated in our mountain range, units of Guerrillas just as the units of

regular troops of General Lacy, armed by Gibraltar, obliged a French military force led by General Boussain to stay in our city. General Boussain was killed by a shot from a highlander in the outskirts of Ronda.

The departure of the French troops in 1812 brought with it the destruction of defensive buildings in Ronda, such as the fort. Flour and oil mills and crops were also destroyed. This caused a very precarious situation for Ronda and its surrounding mountain range where bands of highwaymen and bandits formed and operated on the route from Gibraltar. These existed until the beginning of the **XX** century.

After the difficult situation created by the War of Independence and the absolutist period of Fernando VII our city was blessed with a definite socio-economic improvement. The people from Ronda whose liberal disposition is politically their notable feature actively take part in the dynamics of contemporary history, with its republic, liberal and conservative parties; giving irreproachable tribunes as Rios Rosas, or avant-garde pedagogues such as Giner de los Rios, master of liberal and lay intellectualim and he was the creator of the Institution of Free Education; or becoming the first town in the province of Málaga to have, in 1891, a Municipal Corporation with a Republican majority.

Illustrious visitors are received in Ronda during this complicated XIX century. The Duke and Duchess of Montpensier visit us in the year 1849 and the Empress Eugene of Montijo, widow of Napoleon III in 1877. This century ends with great droughts and tremendous social problems, accompanied by strikes and riots and with a great literary political motivation as the proliferation of local newspapers published during this period prove.

The present century is, for Ronda, a century of future and development, tarnished by the Civil War and the years of precariousness that followed it.

The serious damage caused by the French in our military installations did not allow the city of Ronda to recuperate its traditional military feeling until the end of the last century with the arrival of a cavalry regiment and a battalion of sappers at the beginning of the present century. However our proximity to the Spanish protectorate in the North of Africa involved us completely in the Wars of Morocco until its independence on the 11th. of February 1957. Equally we should mention the ubication in our city of one of the Military Service Instruction Centres (I.P.S) from post-war years to 1972. At the moment the Military Centre is occupied by the 4th. Company of the Spanish Legion (Legion Tercio Farnesio).

Politically, our city has taken part in the majority of things that have taken place in our country this century. Alfonso XIII celebrates his 16th. birthday the17th. of May 1902 and is crowned and acknowledged as King of Spain when he takes an oath on the constitution in force. A kingdom tarnished by strikes, transgressions and the Wars of Morocco broken by the dictatorship of General Primo de Rivera from the 14th. of September 1923 to the 28th. of January 1930. The fall of Primo de Rivera leads us to the proclamation of the Second Republic on the14th. of April 1931. The military uprising of the18th. of July 1936 breaks the democratic period and puts General Franco in power until his death the 20th. of November 1975. Juan Carlos I is proclaimed Constitutional King of Spain the 22nd. of November 1975. Our town has been governed during this last democratic period by a first legislation of coalition and another four of socialist majority.

Socially and economically the XX century started with the opening of the railway line in 1891 and the planning of new roads and the finishing of many local roads. Alfonso XIII visits us the 4th. of March 1909 and inaugurates the Espinel Theatre in May of the same year. He provides funds for

a modern system to supply drinking water to the town, and for a new cemetery. A grand hotel, Hotel Reina Victoria is built. Others built in the same year but now non existent were Royal, Polo, Gibraltar and Del Comercio.

The Caja de Ahorros (or Savings Bank) of Ronda is founded in February 1909 and was the first savings bank in Andalusia, and since the amalgamation the 24th. of February 1990 with other savings banks of Andalusia it is called Unicaja. The first Georgista Spanish-American Congress regarding a sole tax takes place in Ronda in May 1913 and later in 1919 and it was in our city where Andalusia was to settle its foundation with the creation of the coat of arms of Andalusia and its green and white flag. Numerous factories of pork sausage, textiles, furniture and wine makers install themselves here. Numerous cafes and cultural centres open everywhere reflecting an activity typical of a city, where commerce was always the axis of its main occupation controlled by its powerful middle class.

Although the crisis of the fifties brought about a great emigration of the working class, with a resulting reduction of population and negative repercussions in the socio-economic development of the town, it has become in the last decade a service town for the villages and a great tourist industry from which we benefit at the moment.

Gate of Philip V and Old Bridge

As a dream it rises above the abyss. The rock along the Guadalevín (Wadi-al-Laban - deep river), is caressed and its fringe of crystal clear water sweeps away fantasies and aspirations of a great live history, allowing all sadness to die and letting all anxiety fly away. The fertile nature which is born each day by the Hidalga, and dies near San Cristóbal,to be reborn each day with its turban of glory and vanity, to be loved and desired, because anyone who knows you, ¡Oh Ronda !, falls in love with you.

Deep thoughts have been dedicated to you.They call you The Beautiful Veiled Woman, and between fantasies and realities, they have paid compliments to you. "Ronda, high and deep, categorical, profound, round and tall", Juan Ramón Jiménez said. "You are like a furtive air" Antonio Gala. In order to know her, the ideal guide is "The Mute Cicerone" According to Eugenio D`Ors, "Because in her, silence is history". Rafael Alberti while exiled in Rome, remembered his Spain and the bullfighting and in 1967 thinking of Ronda and a bullfighter who was a native of Ronda, Antonio Ordóñez, thought that when he (Ordóñez) fought the bulls "Angels with bells would kick up a hell of a row in order to see him" and he dedicated to him and to his father "Chuflillas del Niño de la Palma". The great poet with the andaluz soul, Federico García Lorca, could not forget our town in one of his most important works, Mariana Pineda, IV scene, estampa I, he reminds us "¿Shall I bring you a book? Bring her The Bull Ring from illustrious Ronda. ¿ Where you at the bullfighting ? ¡He was! In the most important bullfight of Ronda la Vieja . Five jet black bulls, with green and black rosettes fixed to their neck. I thought always of you, I thought, if only my sad friend were with me, my Marianita Pineda ..."; Gerardo Diego gets great pleasure when they pay compliments to you in "The Plaza of Ronda" "My pure Ronda, Plaza of light without a fair, rose that lasts"; Dionisio Ridruejo in "A walk in the afternoon" or José María Pemán in " Ronda and the poet" and so many others that looked at you and painted you or sketched you, as, for instance the great Japanese master Togo Seije or the British impressionist David Bomberg. Romantics like Gustave Doré or David Roberts left their mark on your stones and paths. Let us not forget the contemporary traveller James A. Michener and many more who with their pens have made us delight with your beauty, your uniqueness and your charms, as James Joyce who finished his masterpiece Ulysses in Ronda: "Ronda and the old windows... the gardens of the Alameda, yes and all the strange little back streets indeed... and the gardens of roses, jasmine, geraniums and cactus". Prosper Mérimée with a native girl of Ronda creates a myth "Carmen of Ronda" and Rainer María Rilke with his "Spanish Trilogy" and "Epistolary" manifests when he wrote to his friend the Sculptor Rodin from the Hotel Reina Victoria of this town: "Ronda, where I am at this moment is an incomparable region of rock that carries on its shoulders a little town, whitened and rewhitened with lime". The great traveller and author Ernest Hemingway always had a passage or thought for our beloved town in everything he wrote on Spain. He writes in " Death in the afternoon ": " Ronda really is a beautiful place. It has been built in a circle of mountains on top of a plateau. That´s where you should go, if you ever go to Spain... ". Washington Irving in "Tales of the Alhambra "refers to Ronda" They had the same charming look that I have found in the elegant highlanders of Ronda"; and finally so as not to continue with a never ending list of quotations, a thought for that universal character Orson Welles, who by his own will, decided to have his ashes left in the place which he considered to be the ideal haven for someone so versatile and ingenious.

After travelling through our orography, through the annals of the history and literature we go into the town, letting ourselves be overcome by the silence, by its charm, by our fantasy, in and out of the little back streets and little corners, amongst coats of arms and lintels, surrounded by grills and geraniums, we discover, despite the many changes which have taken place during the last years, one of the most important and best preserved Historic-Artistic Collections of Spain.

< Gate of Philip V   Casa Don Bosco. Gardens >

< Church of Santa María Mirhab

*I*n the Urban district of the old town, the most representative open area was always the Main Square or the City Square, or as it is called today The Square of the Duchess of Parcent. Under Arab rule this square of the large market place had an irregular shape, more or less trapezoidal, and included the most representative buildings of the town: The Principal Mosque or Aljama, Main Market, Jail and Castle. After the Christian conquest of the 22nd. of May 1485, they served practically the same purposes: Parish Church, Town Hall and Jail, the Corn exchange, Castle and also shops.

It was in this place that the three main functions of every medieval city were represented: Religion, Justice and the Army, and we now have a complex of linked monuments that fascinate everyone who sees them.

Enlarged at the end of the XIXth. century, with its present aspect, and embellished by the Duchess of Parcent with the actual gardens. Hidden from us by the constant watch of the cedars, cypresses, palms and laurels, is the monument to our famous native of Ronda, **Vicente Espinel** (1550 - 1624) author, poet and musician. He was a friend of Lope de Vega (1562 - 1635) who called him Maestro, and of Miguel de Cervantes (1547 - 1616). His musical facet is unknown by many, but it was he who added the 5th cord, that is called prima to the Spanish guitar. As a poet he was the creator of the tenth octosyllabic, poetic composition that from him gets its name "Espinela". As a writer he was the author of one of the masterpieces of Spanish literature in our Golden Century, the picaresque novel "El Escudero Marcos de Obregón". Finally, worthy of mention is the creator of such beautiful gardens, the architect Jean Claude Forestier of Paris, designer of so many other beautiful gardens in Europe, such as the María Luisa Park in Seville, the Boulogne Woods in Paris, or the gardens of our House of the Moorish King.

In this great monumental fusion the most representative building of the square, inhaling cathedral air from any angle is the interesting and mysterious **Church of our Lady of the Incarnation.**

Erected in the highest part of the town, in the same place where, according to tradition, a Roman temple to Julius Caesar's memory was built. Nothing remains of the temple except what were, possibly, the foundations and a plaque, to which historians made reference until recently, and in which one could read IULIO DIVO MUNICIPES. Made to commemorate the victory of this illustrious statesman over the sons of Pompey, Gnaeus and Sextus in the battle of Munda 45 B.C. and marked peace after so many years of civil wars prolonged by outstanding men of the Empire.

At the end of the XIth. century the Arabs built, over the ruins of the temple and of a Visigoth church constructed at a later date, an Aljama or main mosque, whose present remains are only the location of the Mudejar tower, today a bell tower, and remains of the arch of the mihrab with part of a wall on the back of the present sanctuary. An altar decorated with plant designs as well as geometric and calligraphic designs from the Nasrid Dynasty, from the end of the XIIIth. century, beginning of the XIVth. that remind us of the Alhambra of Granada.

After the Conquest of Ronda, the Main Mosque was consecrated by the senior Chaplain of the Army of Fernando the Catholic King, Don Pedro de Toledo, under the advocation of Our Lady of the Incarnation, to whom Queen Isabel had a great devotion .

Gothic capital detail. Interior of Santa María

King Fernando granted it the category of Abbey and Carlos I granted other favours, amongst them he named it the Main Church "ad instar cathedralis hispalensis"; with honours and prayers as those stipulated for cathedrals, its chapter having the power to name the parish priests of Ronda, Arriate, Cuevas del Becerro and Serrato. All of this until the Concordat of 1851 between Pope Pious IX and Queen Isabel II when it was reduced to the category of Suprimida Collegiate Church with the rank of Main Parish Church .

A highlight of the façade is the bell tower of Mudejar style in uncovered brickwork. Built on top of the foundation of the old minaret of the mosque it has been restored on many occasions after being hit by lightening in 1523 and after the earthquake of 1580. The ground plan is square with four main parts superimposed and particularly worthy of mention is the upper area of the third part which is octagonal in shape and communicates with the belltower, ending up with a gothic crenelation and the fourth part, also octagonal, decorated with glazed hemispheres. Finally, at the top of the tower, a small circular shaped cupola, covered in blue and white tiles from the XVIIIth. century.

On the left, at the base of the bell tower, The little Tower House, a charming Mudejar building that used to be a little chapel or oratory cut off from the main building, which has various little roofs at different heights and directions, and some beautiful blind horseshoe arches on the front.

On the right, hiding the main door of the original gothic church from which a pointed arch is noticed, are some beautiful rows of balconies, built during the reign of Felipe II, to be used as boxes, from which the nobility and authorities of the town could watch the jousts, bullfighting and the public acts. Towards 1570 the Correjidor (Mayor) of Ronda, Alonso de Espinosa y Calderón, ordered continuous balconies to be made throughout the plaza. The work was finished in time for the fiestas which celebrated the birth of Felipe III in 1578. Afterwards, they elaborated by making the actual galleries on the façade of the Church, after the restoration works carried out following the earthquake of 1580.

The little house by the tower. Santa María

Santa María Church among palms and cedar trees >

Santa María is a church worth visiting. A religious building that little by little shows you its small treasures as a clear example of a town and its social evolution. It is really the most representative building of our religious architecture where two different periods and two architectural styles harmonize.

Its gothic nave is built at the end of the XVth. century and beginning of the XVth. It is late gothic with 3 separate naves with pointed arches and columns with different heights in their bases and one single continuous capital. The decoration of these capitals is not uniform and has designs of thistles, fantasy animals and even anthropomorphous figures, as one can appreciate in those which frame the choir.

The earthquake of 1580 badly affected the structure of the nave, and this is why the central nave, covered originally by a Mudejar coffered ceiling, is substituted by four hemispherical vaults over pendentives with motives of the lauretanas litanies .

The height of the vaults is reduced and the side walls are re-inforced with relieving arches making the most of the preserved Gothic arches already there, and the newly constructed semicircular arches to take in the side altars.

Here we have the Chapel altar, beautiful and baroque which was covered in gold ,in situ, in the last part of the XVIIIth. century . Four Salomonic columns, decorated with motives of vines and fruits, frame the three parts that the main altar is divided into. In the centre, at the base, El Sagrario sculptured in gold plated wood. Above it, a little niche houses the fine and carefully made carving of Santa Ana and the Virgin child by an unknown author. The central part is framed by two false pillars decorated with garlands, that support a beautifully embellished semicircular arch where the niche is found .-What an exquisite baroque image with a tiny waist and pompous mantel in the breeze.- On the sides of the altar, the statues of St. Rafael and St. Joachim without sculptural value. And crowning the altars a high relief flanked by two small Salomonic columns, representing the Mystery of the Incarnation.

To the left, the retable of the Virgin of Sorrows, that used to be the Altar of Relics of which only one relic is preserved and is kept in the Museum-Exposition of the Sacristy of this church and which we shall visit at the end. The gold plated altar of churrigueresque style is divided into three parts with an elaborate side decoration. A large opening with a semicircular arch, forms the recess where the Statue of Our Lady of Sorrows, according to some made by Martínez Montañés and to others by María Luisa Roldán "La Roldana". The latter being the most general opinion. Finally, one can see that it is completed by a semicircular crenellation that covers a large panel with the attributes of the Passion of Our Lord.

To the right, a fresco of St. Christopher by the local painter José de Ramos; signed in 1798. It reminds us of the great paintings of this saint existing in the Spanish Cathedrals.

Our attention is drawn to the modern painting in the side arches. They are by Raymonde Pagégie, a painter born in Paris but resident in Madrid. The tremendous humidity of the walls prevented the artist from painting al fresco and so she decided to paint them in oils. They represent scenes from the Life of St. Peter, the Fall of St. Paul, the Vision of the Apocalypse, the Crucifixion and the Last Supper and they were done between 1982 and 1988. One can see how the author has wanted

Choir. Santa María

Renaissance Nave. Iglesia de Santa Maria >
Canopy. Santa Maria >>

< Santa Maria. Galleries

Collegiate Church of Our Lady of the Incarnation

to reflect the ingenuity of Gothic painting, altering perspective and even some of her sketchings are almost childlike. She shows her originality in the presentation of the horsemen - trotting and not galloping - and in the three crucifixions,and in the painting of the Last Supper, divided into two, the Candelabra of seven branches represents the announcement of the partition and the separation of the Jewish people.

We could continue being more explicit in our visit but in order not to become tired we shall continue with the new church, but before, see on the wall at the back of the choir there is a statue of Our Lady Immaculate, Queen of Families by Antonio J. Lubé de Luque, one of the most prestigious image makers of Seville today. This is the first image of the Virgin, in the whole world, that is dedicated to Our Lady under this advocation, and at present, the last invocation of the litanies in the Holy Rosary.

The new church or Renaissance nave, as it is incorrectly called, as even though it was started with that architectural style the finishing touches were extremely Baroque. It is an architectural marvel the way the joining up of two churches with two styles has been solved. The embedded half columns, Gothic and Renaissance make the transition from one church to the other a surprise, but it will not be disagreeable to you.

After the earthquake of 1580, when the north and west parts of the church were destroyed, it was decided to enlarge it and to build a church which would be a replica, or resemblance, to the cathedrals of Granada and Málaga, in Renaissance style with Corinthian and Tuscan columns and it took from 1584-1704 to build it.

The influence of Diego de Siloé, put into practice by his pupil Andrés de Vandelvira in several towns of Andalusia is felt, in respect to the proportions between diameter and height of

< Altar of the Tabernacle. Sta. María

Ceiling of the City Hall, XVI th. century

the columns, which in order to obtain a greater height without breaking up the proportion, are crowned with an entablature, that in turn goes around the perimeter of the nave.

This part of the church is formed by a nave of a basilical ground plan with a central vault and five side vaults. The central nave is covered with a ribbed vault and its centre by a segment of a sphere with eight ribs and a great central medallion; in the pendentives another four medallions that represent the Evangelists. The aisles are covered also with a barrelled vault but in transversal direction and the chapels with a quarter sphere where boxed ribs appear in the shape of keys that remind us of the decoration of the Cathedral of Málaga, but without the gold leaf of the latter.

The church has four doors, two that give entrance to the first church and the other two open two niches in the new part. The niches entrance of the Evangelists in the old part has a semicircular arch between pilasters crowned by a divided pediment and pyramids with a niche in the centre. The Epistles Gate dates back to 1766 and is the same plan as the latter, but with the anagram of Our Lady on the keystone and a great profusion of rosettes in its decoration. The entrances of the new church both present the same characteristics. The access arch is framed by some very thick pilasters and venerated niches, but the door of the Epistle has two figures of winged lions in the spandrels, from whose tongues animals are suspended. The eaves of the old part of the church are very interesting and represent heads of a monstrous type with a great medieval style.

A splendid lamp of wrought iron made by Antonio Aguilera, a local artist of Ronda and inaugurated on the feast of the Immaculate Conception in 1994 hangs from the central vault. He took four months to make the lamp and 480 kilos of iron were used. The mounting of the glass-24.870 pieces- is the work of José Antonio Tirado García and of Vicente Becerra Cabrera, and the design was an idea of the parish priest Don Gonzalo Huesa Lope. It measures ten metres.

We begin with the altar of Saint John of God in the Evangelists part of the church. It belonged to the old chapel of Peace and Charity, of the Hospital of the Catholic King and Queen which no longer exists. It is of Baroque style and in its sanctuary is a relic of St. John of God and in the niche of the saint is a beautiful statue of Our Lady of the Light by an unknown artist from the XVIth. century. A small vault which contains an extremely valuable carving of St. Peter of Verona crowns the altar.

Following is the altarpiece of the Sacred Heart of Jesus, the old altar from Our Lady of the Angels. The canopy over the main altar used to be part of it. It is a delicately worked object in Canadian red pine wood with a centre panel that surrounds the carving of the Sacred Heart, by the Madrilenian R. Font, acquired after the Civil War in 1940, when the Salesians still ran the parish. On the sides of the altarpiece are statues of St. Peter and St. Paul, of little value .

Next comes the present altar of Our Lady of Grace that was dedicated to Our Lady of Greater Sorrow until its transfer to the old Altar of Relics, its actual position. On the altar is a statue of Our Lady of Grace, patron saint of the local Equestrian Society of Spanish Noblemen who brought it here from the hermitage in the district of San Francisco. It is withhout doubt one of the oldest images that is venerated in Ronda.

Our Lady of Sorrows. Santa María

The altar matches the one on the other side of the Main Altar with the difference that this one is gold plated. The altar is in three parts. The central part stands out due to a niche with a glass door where we find the alcove of Our Lady.

But the most outstanding of all is the canopy of the main altar. It formed part of the Altar of Our Lady of the Angels until it was brought to this important place to occupy the void left on the main altar, after the Civil War. It is the work of Esteban de Salas, 1727.

Four beautiful pillars flanked on each side by pedestals which are delicately carved in filigree and support a large vaulted dome, with bulls-eye windows in each oval, forming the canopy. It is crowned by a small octagonal temple which is intensely decorated. It is all carved in filigree from red pine wood by unknown artists but attributed by some to the monks. The truth is that each rose, each detail, each vase on the top part is, in itself, a work of art that makes it a masterpiece, and focus of attention of all visitors.

Worth of mention at the same time is the sanctuary, a real jewel of the XVIIIth. century by the goldsmith Vergara from Málaga. The front panel of the altar is made in white metal in the workshop of Gonzalo Angulo, from Lucena, as are all the candlesticks that decorate the altar.

Next we have the Altar of the Virgin of La Cabeza that matches with that of Our Lady of Grace. Its image, brought back after the Civil War, is a beautiful carving from the XVIIIth. century. It is venerated in this church from the

beginning of September until the second Sunday of June when it is taken by pilgrimage to the hermitage of the Caves of St. Antón.

The sacristy is a nave with barrelled vault added to the Church in the XVIIIth. century without an outside door. This was opened in 1894 on the occasion of the Beatification of Friar Diego José of Cádiz. Inside is the little Parish Museum where we can admire, together with some sacred ornaments, several chalices and sacred vases from various periods, Gregorian chant choir books from the XVIth. century and the two Constitutional Books of the church from 1504 - 1723.

Now we have the altar of San Antonio that belonged also, to the Church of Peace and Charity from the old Hospital of Santa Barbara. It is a simple altar piece, widely decorated in stone with crenellation that encloses a symbolic sun with the hearts of Jesus and Mary. The statue of the saint has no value.

And to end our visit its splendid Choir. Finished in 1736 in a manneristic baroque style.

City Hall. Interior

The lower stalls, in walnut, have 12 seats of honour with the backs carved with the symbols of the litanies of the Virgin Mary and the top part in cedar wood is made up of 24 seats with the backs carved representing the Sacred Heart, Apostles and Saints.

Some of the figures of the saints are completely new, restored by the local artist L. Sánchez . One can clearly see the difference between the originals and the substitutes by the different depth of the gouge. During the Civil War the bas-relief of the Incarnation and Calvary that made up the central part and some figures in the main body were lost. Also, of the organ of two pieces, constructed in 1710, only the cabinet of one of the boxes remains.

There are no records as to who created the choir. Ronda always had a great tradition in wood carving and there is nothing to stop us thinking that this was the work of local artists. In the middle is a walnut lectern made by Vicente Becerra Jiménez who used to be the Sacristan of this church, with four Gregorian chant choir books from the XVIth. century made in parchment, illuminated and polychromed and of great artistic value.

We leave the church through the door of the Little Sacristy. Next to it, the Baptismal Font of little artistic value, but of great historic value because some very important local people have been baptised in it, such as Antonio Ordóñez.

Leaving the church of Our Lady, we come back into the plaza and find before our eyes the solid, elegant building of the old Military Barracks, which is now the Town Hall of Ronda. It was built in 1734 to house the Number 28 of the Provincial Regiments founded by Felipe V, after leaving the castle which was in continual deterioration brought on by the reconquest. It was built on top of the old shops that occupied the front of the main square, and restored in 1818, following the damage caused by the French. In the rear of the building are the Old Communal Granary, Corn Exchange and the Royal Bakery from the XVIth. century; forming the most important development of the town as integral parts of the actual Municipal Building.

Some years ago these buildings were restored and in 1978 became the new **City Hall** respecting the original aesthetics enriched by a Mudejar coffered ceiling from the XVIth. century, which was donated by the Countess of Santa Pola and embellished the main entrance stairway. The entrance composed of a door whose lintel corresponds to the last restoration and between pillars it has on the left side the coat of arms with the chalice and the star of the city of Cuenca, twin town of Ronda by agreement of both municipals in 1975; on the right

City Hall. Meeting Hall

Bell Tower of Santa Isabel Convent

side is the coat of arms of our town, granted by the Catholic Monarchs. Worth visiting in this building are the Assembly Hall and the lower floor which used to be the old Corn Exchange.

Continuing along this pavement we have a white building with the coat of arms of the Catholic Monarchs on its façade. This is the Magistrates Court for Ronda and its district. It was the first Town Hall and Jail after the Christian Reconquest, following the ordinance of the King and Queen that provided, for the Main Square the Town Hall, the Jail, Local Government and Notaries.

In the middle of the XIXth. century the Town Hall was moved to a new building in the centre of town next to the New Bridge, (today the Plaza de España, and actual building of the National Parador, 1994), until 1978 when it was transferred yet again to its present situation in this square. The jail, on the contrary, still occupied this building until the end of 1950.

According to legend, contrary to historic reality, the building where Doña Margarita of Austria stayed when she came to enjoy the seigniory of Ronda on the death of her husband Prince Don Juan, heir to the Catholic Monarchs. His premature death caused so much pain that the King and Queen decided to chan-

City Hall and Church of Our Lady of Succour

ge the colour of mourning in their Kingdoms, which was white, to black which is still used today.

At the back of the square, surrounded by gardens, acacias and cedres, the **Church of Our Lady of Help,** (María Auxiliadora) from 1955 which has a great local devotion and great Marian tradition whose school of the Sacred Heart of Jesus, founded by the Marquis of Moctezuna, is built on top of the ruins of **the old Laurel Castle** whose construction was ordered at the beginning of the IInd. century B. C. by General Scipio Eamilianus on finalizing the pacification and control of the Celtiberian tribes of the area.

It was used by the Visigoths as a castle and by the Arabs as a fort and was then used by the Christians after the reconquest of the city, despite its state of ruin and the great damage and deterioration suffered through the centuries, caused by earthquakes and the abandonment of it. The French repaired it to house some of their troops in Ronda, but the 26th. of August 1812 the French governor gave order to dynamite it and other buildings of military interest in the area. This sudden abandonment of the town by the French army, took with it the des-

truction of all the military armament stored and the demolition of the building itself, almost making it totally disappear together with the Gate of the Images; a Roman gate that gave access to the fort and main district from the Top (or High) district and Gate of Almocábar.

Having fun

Sword mould, Sa-Idda type. Palace Mondragón

stone façade with semicircular arches is finished off with the coat of arms of the Franciscans in its keystone and is accompanied by a charming bell tower crowned by a roof of Arab tiles with four slopes.

On the other side of the church is the convent with a stone lintel and the Franciscan coat of arms over its door. The building was greatly restored in 1952. At the moment it is a shrine dedicated to St. Nicholas with many visitors, on Mondays of each week that have a tremendous devotion to him.

On the other side of the square we have the **Church of Charity** from the XVIth. century founded by a local man called Pedro de Miranda who gave his worldly goods to the Order of Charity so that they could pay for the burial of homeless people and those without families and also so that young orphan girls would have a dowry on marriage. Today it is occupied by the nuns of Sister Angela of the Cross.

The façade is made from mock brick and its doorway of stone with semicircular arch stands out, crowned by a split pediment and finished off with a cross. At the back of this building there used to be a house where poor travellers were taken in and given lodgings.

To go into the street of Manuel Montero is to discover the charm of the old town; it was the old main road of the silk merchants district and first royal street after the Christian Conquest. The beauty of the old fortification walls and an ancestral home from 1616, accompanied by beautiful balconies with bird cage grills, we arrive in front of **Mondragón Palace** which is made of stone. It is a noblemans house, surrounded by a festoon of white houses and orange trees that make up the plaza of the same name.

It was originally the residence of King Abomelik from the Banu Marin tribe. He was the son of the Emperor of Fez and was King of Ronda and Algeciras at the beginning of the

This short period of Napoleonic occupation gave way to a very beautiful story of Carmen of Ronda, immortalised by the French author, Prosper Mérimée.

At the end of the XIXth. century the land was acquired by the Moctezuma Foundation, for the construction of a teaching centre, work which has continued to date by the Salesian Order.

Closing the square are two religious buildings; the Church and Convent of St. Isabel of the Angels and the Church of Charity.

The **church and convent of St. Isabel of the Angels**, Sisters of the Order of St. Clare were constructed in 1540 by Don Luís de Oropesa and Doña Catalina de Triviño, on the plot which was occupied by the jail and the water tank during Islamic domination.

The church, with only one nave, continuing with the choir was covered by a Mudejar coffered ceiling which was hidden by Baroque elements at the end of the XVIIth. century. Its

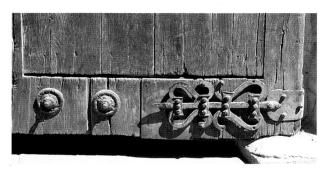

Mondragón Palace. Ironwork in Ronda

XIVth. century. After the fall of the Banu Marin and the union of our small kingdom with the Nasrid dynasty of Granada, the building became the residential palace of Hamed El Zegrí who was the last Arab Governor of the town. After the reconquest of the town and following the parcelling of the land by royal warrant in 1491, the house was ordered to be handed over to Captain Mondragon by the personal guard of King Fernando. Later it was occupied by the King himself in the year 1501 due to the uprising of the Moors in these mountains.

Later the property changed hands and went to the Valenzuela family. One of its members, the first Marquis of Villasierra, was the favourite of Mariana of Austria who was the widow of Felipe IV. He was also a favourite of Carlos II but he fell into disgrace and later died in exile in Mexico

This palace is the most important of the civil architecture of our town. In its asymmetry and walls the changes and restorations of the last centuries can be perfectly seen. The layout of the gardens and the entrance to the corridor that still joins it to the old fortress are preserved from the Muslim building.

The monumental façade of sandstone has two pairs of Doric columns from the XVIth. century in the lower part that support a second body of pure style from the XVIIth. century. There is a balcony in the centre whose opening is flanked by Ionic columns in whose tympanum is a small niche. A doorway whose iconology centres on the attributes or ejaculations of the Virgin Mary; Marian elements that are repeated in the house of Ruiz in this same street, Manuel Montero.

The main façade is flanked by two Mudejar towers, like observation towers, in mock brick-work and semicircular arches crowned by a roof with four slopes. Its studded door gives way to a beautiful hall embellished with a great Mudejar coffered ceiling from the XVIth. century in cedar wood, followed by the enclosure of the stables and a stone bench or step to help the ladies mount their horse, remind us of the architectural elements from our Spanish Golden Century. In the interior is the present **Municipal Archaelogical museum**. We should point out, apart from the ornamental mixture of Mudejar- Renaissance elements, the display of interesting pieces from the Stone and Metal Age, such as the mould for forging swords of bronze of the Sa Idda style, from the VIIth.

century B.C, found in the local fields and the very valuable and large example of Muslim funeral systems in Andalusia.

Its first patio, or patio of the well from the XVIIIth. century leads us to what is known as the Mudejar patio; the most important in the palace with brick semicircular arches decorated with Renaissance tiles that support a wooden gallery whose walls still have part of Renaissance frescoes with which the building was decorated in the XVIth. century by Melchor de Mondragón.

Going through a horseshoe arch we come to the garden whose silence, broken only by the musical sounds from its fountains, takes us into the atmosphere of the culture of Moorish Andalusia, complimented by the enormity of its environs and in the background the whiteness of the district of San Francisco hurts our eyes.

The Mudejar covered ceiling of the noble drawing room and the vault of the main stairway decorated with polychromed heraldic motives of the family are worthy of note.

We continue our walk along Gameros and arrive at the house of Martos, a modernist building from the beginning of this century and constructed on top of the old Arab walls of the Albacara. The charming garden of Campillo,

Mondragón Palace. Well

∧ *XVI th. century Patio.*   *Mondragón Palace.*   *XVIII th. century Patio.* ∨   *Gardens >*

San Juan Bosco. Patio

María Auxiliadora Square will open our eyes to one of the most impressionable views of the modern town. The Parador on our right is where bravery of being on top of the abyss starts, as if galloping along the rocky mass that supports it, to continue with the gardens of the Alameda and finish up at the end with the Victorian building of the Hotel Reina Victoria built in 1906. Here the monument to Rainer María Rilke observes impassive the evenings of San Cristóbal as the fading rays of the sun delight us on bidding Good-bye at the end of the day.

From this little square we start descending to the old Albacara (Gate of the Wind), Gate of Christ and the old mills of the Gorge.

The ramparts of the Albacara are situated to the west of the town where the precipice reaches a depth of 100 mts. They were made with mortar at the end of the XIIIth. century, forming part of the natural defensive system made by the gorge in this area. They adapt to the terrain, spanning crags and slopes so that it was not necessary to build towers. Their good preservation meant there was no necessity for reconstruction over the centuries until the French occupation in 1810 when they were restored. The vital function for the survival of the city is reflected clearly in the ramparts and in their restored gates.

They defended all the area that is now called Campillo, between the Gate of Los Molinos (the mills) and the Gate of Viento (the wind) extending to a great exterior rampart until the actual ramparts of the South of the Alcazaba. The object of this external enclosure was to create a second exterior rampart and to give the Albacara its correct use as in other great forts of Muslim Spain. It was a place to enclose the cattle of the area when the danger alarm was given if the city was to be attacked.

Its exterior entrances were **The Gate of the Wind** with a segmental arch of bricks that

communicated the Valley of the Potros with the main district by a steep slope and is today one of the most pleasant walks in our visit of Ronda, and **The Gate of the Mills** (also known as the Arch of Christ) gives access to the bottom of the gorge where for centuries, farmers and labourers worked in the flour and oil mills, grinding and pressing. This entrance of rubble work is formed by three arches. The two outer ones are horseshoe shaped and the centre one stilted semicircular with open space in front of it.

It takes the name Arch of Christ due to a little shrine encrusted into the right side of the entrance where the workers of the mills, oil presses and electricity stations in the bottom of the gorge kept their patron saint

San Juan Bosco. Fireplace

Christ Crucified where a little lamp was always lit before the feet of the statue until the mills were abandoned about 1955.

Returning to the plaza, surrounded by almonds and vines during the whole of our uphill walk, a stop from time to time becomes necessary in order to recuperate peace and tranquillity and to be able to look back and enjoy the indescribable beauty around us. We arrive back to the Plaza and continue along Tenorio St. as far as number 20. The visit of this **house of Saint John Bosco** will once again fill our eyes with gorgeous treasure that nature has given us from the unique location of this little palace.

Modernist style, constructed at the beginning of this century, it belonged to a family called Granadinos

New Bridge and Parador

whose last wishes were that the house should be used by the Salesian Brothers as a rest home for aged and sick priests of that order. It has a beautiful patio decorated with Nasrid tiles and a very complete representation of regional ceramics. We should mention, apart from the XIXth. century tapestries, the furniture in walnut, where the chimney from the main drawing room is the most clear example of Rondan art in the most pure Castillian style. Continuing , a visit to the garden is a must: an orchard on the very edge of the precipice, tended with care by the long lived Salesian Don Julián de Vicente y Milanés. It hangs in space by the wim of human wishes and has us facing the most representative, monument of our town **"The New Bridge".**

The Bridge of Ronda, as people call it, is close to the Bull Ring, the heart and soul of our town. There were two great projects to make this bridge. The first in the year 1735, period of Felipe V that consisted of a great arch, 35 mts. diameter, whose work took only eight months but it collapsed six years later in 1741, and in this catastrophe 50 people died.

A few years later, in 1751 work was started again and the construction was finally finished in 1793 coinciding with the Royal fair of May,

which means that it took 42 years to complete. The architect in charge of this construction was Don José Martín Aldehuela, an Aragones architect from the town of Manzanera in the province of Teruel.

This great work is 98 mts. high and built in ashlars. Its foundations start at the bottom of the gorge and it is in 3 sections. The bottom part is formed by a semicircular arch, above which there is a central arch that reaches 90 mts. with two smaller side arches that support the surface at street level. In the central part there is a room which measures approximately 60 square mts and has had several uses in its 200 long years of history. It has mostly been known as a jail for dangerous prisoners and those condemned to death. Its original entrance was from the square building on its right which was used as a control tower.

In the constitution of such a symbolic work we should also specially mention Juan Antonio Díaz Machuca from Ronda who invented several machines or apparatus which facilitated taking materials down to the bottom of the Gorge and whose inventions were crucial for the construction of such a magnificent building. Finally, to put stop to the legend that the architect com-

mitted suicide or fell into the void once work was completed, we should clarify that Don José Martín Aldehuela, after finishing his work, went to Málaga, where he died in 1802 at the age of 80 and is buried in the Parish of Santiago, in Málaga.

Let us leave this delightful house and continue to the right. Another little square appears before us from where we can see the unusual façade of the **Church of Our Lady of Peace** and the stately home where Friar Diego José de Cádiz died the 24th. of March 1801.

In this church the Patron Saint of Ronda is worshipped. This is the oldest image of the town. Already in the XVIth. century the devotion to this image was practised by the people in the church of San Juan de Letrán, one of the collations founded by the Catholic Monarchs, situated in the actual square of Campillo, but not existing any more. The tradition of this veneration goes back to the time of Alfonso XI. who, after abandoning the attack on the city left an image under this advocation for the Mozarabs although this present one is from the end of the XVIIth. century.

The present temple, from the end of the XVIIth. century and beginning of the XVIIIth.,

consists of just one nave, whose Mudejar coffered ceiling was covered by a baroque barrelled vault, with a hemispherical cupola above the presbytery and a small dome with a lantern. All of the church is covered with abundant decoration that makes it one of the most beautiful baroque buildings of Ronda.

Behind its Churriqueresque altar of carved wood, mirrors and stone chippings we find the artistic alcove with wall paintings of the Virgin of Peace, patron saint and perpetual mayoress of our town since 1947. At the feet of the Virgin, a silver urn containing the remains of Blessed Friar Diego José de Cádiz.

Its façade is from the end of the XVIth. century with a doorway of stone and semicircular arch finished off with a bell gable from the XVIIIth. century. This facade has an embossed decoration of rosettes and stars from the XVIIIth. century that draws our attention for its colours and carvings.

In this church Christ of the Blood is venerated and the statue which dates back to the beginning of the XVIIIC is by the famous sculptor from Seville, Duque Cornejo, author of the choir of the Cathedral of Córdoba and an image of Ecce Homo from the school of Granada.

RONDA,

DIVINE DAWN

OF LIFE

ACCOMPANIED BY

THE RUSTLE OF

THE LEAVES ON

THE TREES,

STIRRED BY

THE BREEZE

FROM THE TAJO

AND RESTRAINED

BY THE MUSIC

OF THE FOUNTAINS.

THE AUTHOR

House of Saint John Bosco. Gardens

Our Lady of Peace. Holy Patron saint of Ronda

In the square, the statue in bronze of Blessed Diego, by Francisco Parra, placed here in commemoration of the centenary of his beatification and with a Papal blessing from His Holiness Legate Mario Tagliaferri.

To the right, continuing along José María Holgado Street we arrive at the **Giants House**, name given to this house by the locals for having on the façade, the sphinx of a Melkar (a Punic Hercules) whose cyclopean shape makes it look like a giant. It was discovered in the district of San Francisco and placed here at the end of the XVIth. century.

This building constructed at the beginning of the XIVth. century in the splendid period of the Banu Marin King Abomelik is one of the most significant examples of the Arab middle class palaces preserved in our town. Its interior has a central patio with a well, surrounded by columns with two rooms where one can see remains of the vegetal decorations in walls, arches and spandrels that remind us of the Alhambra of Granada.

Also, we can appreciate in its interior the different restorations made later due to the different uses of the building, e.g. as the home of the Mayor Ruiz Gutiérrez Escalante and later as a home for abandoned children until the end of the XVIIIth. century.

We return to Tenorio St. but not without first noticing the group of **ancestral houses** that make up this part of the town. Further on, one can see in this same street the old palace of the Marquis of Amarillas and Duke of Ahumada, Viceroy in Nueva España and founder of the Civil Guards. In front of the little palace of the Hinojosas Bohórquez and in this same square, the palace of the Marquis of Moctezuma, heirs to the Ovalles, the building that was occupied by José Bonaparte during his visit to Ronda and which is now the school of St. Teresa of Jesus.

Palaces, mansions, and stately homes form the most important urbanistic development of all Andalusia and one of the best preserved.

The altitude of 780 mts. above sea level gives our town a very cold climate in winter and a very pleasant one in summer, with practically two seasons in the year passing from one to the other very easily but in spring the fresh evenings and dry air were considered to be the best conditions to fight against chest complaints which used to be quite common amongst the infantile population and the main reason why our city was, during a long period, the court of Lower Andalusia, where courtesans and the bourgeois class came looking for tranquillity and the good climate that Ronda offered.

∧ *Typical Patio. XVIIIth.*

House of Martos ∨

House of the Hinojosas Bohórquez. Patio

Once again in Tenorio St. and at the end of it, almost at the bridge and with the Plaza de España in the background we come to **the Convent of Santo Domingo.**

Founded by the Catholic Monarchs immediately after the conquest of Ronda, the patronage of its chapel and convent was given to the Dominican monks, dedicated to St.Peter the Martyr.

Because of its early construction we can appreciate that it is a hybrid of Gothic, Mudejar and Renaissance. Elements of the original building are still remaining: the church but without worship,and parts of the cloisters with some of the cells and passageways on the north side facing the gorge.

The entrance to the church is from the street called Santo Domingo; it is simple and made from stone and in the façade there are

two coats of arms, that of the Dominican Order and that of the Holy Office as it was in this convent that the Inquisition was held. It has three naves with an elevated half orange shape, and a particularly beautiful polychromed coffered ceiling and a choir from the XVIth. century.

We should also mention the social importance that it represents as it was a burial place for important families of Ronda; amongst those is the mausoleum of Don José of Moctezuma y Rojas, located in what used to be the Rosary Chapel.

This building after being abandoned by the Dominicans in their alienation had several different uses; it became cavalry barracks, market or furniture factory.It has recently undergone great restoration works and the building will be put to many different uses for our town.

El Carmen. Typical corner

One doesn't want to leave the town. The bridge awaits us to the right, but we are so enraptured with the old town that it invites us to stay, to continue with our walk and to discover and find out more about the "Beautiful Veiled Woman". Let us walk down the street. **The Museum Palace**, which used to be known as the House of the Guerreros Escalantes (The Escalante Warriors) appears before us as a challenge to our curiosity.

This house with a noble air was built on top of the remains of a little mosque or shrine whose most important remains are found in the lower part of the building, right on the edge of the gorge. In the book which records the distribution of Ronda this spot is mentioned as the place where a small shrine or hermitage was built containing a tomb where the remains of a hermit who had lived a virtuous life were buried on his death. This custom became popular in the XIIIth. and the XIVth. century of the Spanish Islamic period and influenced many believers of the area to bury the faithful this way.

We do not have to go very far before we come to a house which is surrounded by romantic legends and beautiful reality. Hanging from the cliff face (as a pearl mounted in history) admired by all who visit us; it is called **the House of the Moorish King.**

It is not listed as the Royal House in the divisions after the Conquest of Ronda by the Catholic Monarchs. Hernando Del Pulgar, Chronicler of the Kings informs us only and exclusively of the existence of The Mine and our compatriot Vicente Espinel in "The Life of the Hidalgo Marcos de Obregón" refers to it as "One of the most important remains of the Arab Domination in Spain".

This building is from the XVIIIth. century and has changed in structure and ownership over the years, until it reached its present physiognomy thanks to the Duchess of Parcent in the year 1920. The façade has Sevillian tiles that represent a Moorish king, perhaps Abomelik in a hieratic position from which we get the incorrectly named "House of the Moorish King". It is embellished with Rondan forged balconies and Sevillian tiles from this century. The main entrance has double columns and a bare heraldic shield as it would appear that it was the custom for each new owner to apply his own coat of arms on the shield of the previous owner.

Its interior is a labyrinth of rooms, corridors, passages and stairs magnificently embellished by rich wood and the collection of fireplaces installed throughout the building. But what stands out is the main drawing room decorated with Sevillian tiles that represent in the centre the allegories of the periods of man's life: Childhood, Youth and old-Age surrounded by four tiles with themes of flowers, a pomegranate and a quince fruit.

New Bridge and Santo Domingo Convent

Worth visiting are the gardens designed by the French architect Jean Claude Forestier who was also responsible for the famous park of Maria Luisa in Seville. Adapting to the different levels of the rocks they are embelished with lovely Sevillian tiles and Nasrid type fountains of marble. They are complimented at the end with the breathtaking view of the gorge and the Mercadillo. (modern town).

But most worthy of mention is the famous **underground mine.** Built by Abomelik at the beginning of the XIVth. century when Ronda became a natural fortress or bastion between the Arab kingdom of Granada and the Christian kingdom of Seville.

Part of it was built into the live rock and the rest of it in rubblework and bricks with arches and vaults and some windows and hollows to let in the light. The access is through a door in the very gardens of the house from where a staircase starts. It used to have 365 steps although now there are only 200. This is a wonderful feat of engineering and inside one can see several rooms or extensions used as dungeons, a gallery with semicircular arches to store the water and grain and the secret room with a very interesting hemispherical vault that communicated directly to the water supply filled by the flow of the Guadelevin river.

Following the conquest of Ronda more than 300 Christians were freed and their chains were sent, by order of Queen Isabel the Catholic to the church of St. Juan de Los Reyes in Toledo and hung on the façade. From this mine we get the old proverb "In Ronda you could die hauling up water skins".

According to the Chroniclers of the Catholic Monarchs the Christians couldn´t find any more than two other public water supplies in Ronda; that of the Fort where the slaves brought water up from the mine and the deposit of water found in the place where today the

House of the Moorish King. Façade

Museum-Palace of the Counts of Santa Pola

Ronda, Enchanting City

San Sebastian Minaret

convent of Santa Isabel or the Clarisas is situated in the Town Square.

Once again on the hill of Santo Domingo we find ourselves with the dilemma of continuing downhill or going into the narrow street opposite us. We take the Ruedo Doña Elvira. Natural balconies, backstreets, grills and geraniums, trellis or jealousy windows and the shadow of James Joyce in his Ulysses accompany us until we arrive at the charming square of the famous poet from Ronda, Abul Becca.

Here we have **the minaret of Saint Sebastian**, the only minaret preserved in Ronda after the Reconquest and called by this name because the mosque that occupied this site until 1485 was converted into a church and dedicated to Saint Sebastian.

The original construction was completed under Nasrid rule in the XIVth. century and is made in three main parts which are easily recognized: the inside of stone ashlars with a horse shoe door that has a decorated lintel showing an interlaced design in stone and the remains of green glazed ceramics. The central part is a body of mock bricks with two little horseshoe shaped windows on each side with a geometric design of interlaced bricks and finally the high part that corresponds to the Christian period, built as the bell tower for the church with four openings and crowned with a little Mudejar roof with four slopes.

The charm of this street doesn´t finish with the building we have just seen. We continue downhill. To the right the old summer palace of Jalifa of Tetuan during the Spanish Protectorate in the north of Marocco. Birdcages and bulls eyes are the style of grills that accompany us until we come once again into Santo Domingo Street. A new perspective of the Mercadillo appears before us and to the right as though waiting humbly for our arrival is the monumental façade of **the Palace of the Marquis of Salvatierra.**

Situated in one of the most delightful and peaceful corners of the town, a stone cross presides over it and marks the occasion of the conquest of the town by the Marquis of Cádiz. The cross was brought here in 1965 during the restoration of the old quarters by the architect Don Francisco Pons Sorolla, grandson of the great artist of this illustrious surname.

Its baroque façade from 1798 is in stone ashlars. The door has a lintel and Corinthian columns on each side. A beautiful balcony of Rondan wrought iron work made larger by an uneven pediment supported by four bare Indians of colonial influence with a certain

< House of the Moorish King. Gardens

Santa Ana Patio. Mercadillo

mannerism where the boys are mocking and sticking their tongues out while the girls are shy and try to cover the shame caused by their nakedness. Above all of this is the family coat of arms and the head of this family was Vasco Martín de Salvatierra, Contino of the Catholic Monarchs after the Conquest of Granada.

Its interior represents the simplicity of a Rondan house of the XVIIth. and XVIIIth. century with a great central patio embellished with a lovely curb on its well. Remarkable furniture from different periods; some over-ornate XVIIC historical tiles from Seville in the dining-room and a splendid garden with a magnificent example of the Pinsapo Abies complete and justify the visit of this house from which we can see an impressive panorama of the walls of the old Lower district or Jewish quarter, the gates of Xijara and Mancebías, the church of the Holy Spirit, the Arab baths and the Mercadillo or new town.

Continuing downhill we find ourselves at one of the main gates of access to the town, **the Gate of Philip V.**

Following the collapse of the first New Bridge in 1741 it was decided that it was necessary to improve this entrance due to the great influx of people and merchandise that once again were obliged to use it. The old Arab gate of the bridge was substituted by this present one which is much bigger and more convenient. It was made in 1742 during the reign of the first Bourbon on the Spanish throne Philip V and named after him according to the plaque next to the gate.

Formed by a double arch of ashlars, it is topped by three pinnacles and decorated with the shell of Anjou and the Royal coat of arms of the Bourbons on the exterior.

We are not going to leave this inviting corner yet. The view we have through the arch with the new town in the background obliges us to stop and observe that the gate frames one of the most significant views of Ronda where we always find an artist trying to capture such unique charm on his canvas.

Behind us, reserved and silent as though not wanting to bother us, is **the Chapel of the Old Bridge.** A little shrine from the XVIIIth.

century devoted to Mary Immaculate; it is composed of a semicircular arch between pillars with the entrance on the right whose staircase is made from hewn stone.

It corresponds to a series of open shrines built into the walls of Rondan houses and very popular up to the end of the XIXth. century. We have some beautiful examples, such as Our Lord of Forgiveness on Armiñán Street. The Chapel of San Francisco in Espiritu Santo Street, the shrine of San Antonio on the street named after this saint or the niche of the Holy Cross in Marqués de Salvatierra Street.

Continuing downhill we come to **the Old Bridge.** Its origin is Arabic. According to some authors it was built during the reign of Abomelik, King of Ronda, and according to others in the time of Mohammed III of Granada. The truth is that after the conquest of Ronda by the Christians it had to be repaired urgently. In 1616 it was once again destroyed by a flood and reconstructed according to an inscription preserved in its left parapet until the last century that read "*Ronda rebuilt this construction under its joint Corregidor (or Mayor) with*

Salvatierra Palace. Façade

Salvatierra Palace. Patio

Arab baths >

Ronda. Dreamed City

Ronda, a dream City

Marbella, Don Juan Antonio Torrubio de Quiñones for the King Our Lord in the year 1616".

It has only one arch which is 10 mts. diameter and 31 mts. above the level of the river; it is 30 mts. long and 5 mts. wide. In 1961 it was newly restored, little balconies were opened and it was decorated with little balls which give it its actual appearance.

We continue, but we do not cross the bridge. We turn to the right and take the steps that lead us to the Old District or **Jewish Quarters** where the bridge of San Miguel and the Arab Baths are found.

The bridge of San Miguel or the Tannery Bridge is the smallest of all three bridges and is also of Arab origin. Today everyone calls it the Roman Bridge. It is possible that during the Roman occupation a bridge did exist here but the present one is of Islamic construction. It has only one arch which is slightly pointed, of approximately 12 mts. and because of its position it has been damaged several times by the river overflowing. Its actual construction is also from 1961.

Although it is small and appears to be of little importance we should remember that it was the entrance to Ronda from the Old Quarter through the Gates of Xijara and Philip V.

At the end of the narrow staircase that has brought us to this little square we have passed a little hermitage, abandoned and neglected. It is the **Church of The Holy Cross.**

Popular opinion places the synagogue here. Recently many remains and information referring to it have been found but historically we only have knowledge of this chapel after the reconquest of the town, as a sanctuary where workers, masters and proprietors of tanning factories and other industries found in this area showed devotion to the venerable Holy Cross. Also we have knowledge that it was in this small square in front of the chapel where the fiestas of "Los Toros de Fuego" in honour of St. Michael, patron saint of tanners were celebrated. These fiestas are no longer celebrated.

Another edifice, situated in this district of San Miguel or Lower District, worth visiting because it is one of the best preserved of all Spain, is the Arab baths. They were built at the end of the XIIIth. beginning of the XIVth. century next to the stream of Las Culebras, the perfect place for easy water supply. Despite being spoliated, and the gypsium and all the beautiful, rich materials of marble, and mosaics with which they were covered and enriched being stolen they are practically ready to be used with minimum restoration. They were not the only baths in existence during the Islamic domination but the most important.

The building is surrounded by a wall of blind arches and has a tower at the end which had a water wheel (now non existent) that brought the water from the stream, sending it, after, along a small aqueduct supported by arches to the steam baths. The baths consist of three rooms easily recognised by their individual structure.

In the first, "the hot room" was the stove to heat the water that came from the wheel with a chimney for the outlet of smoke; it was practically the service room.

The system used was known as hypocaust, passed down from the Romans, that consisted of the heating of the water in the stove, and the vapour of hot air would then be sent along underground channels to the central room (or chamber). Chimneys were embedded in the walls as outlets for smoke and steam.

The second room, "or central chamber" is divided into three naves covered by hemispherical vaults above brick horseshoe shaped arches. Some of these brick arches and pendentives have been restored but there are some other very interesting elements such as a Roman Corinthian capital which is very eroded. The illumination is provided by star shaped light shafts orientated from east to west so that the sunlight enters perfectly every hour of the day and their magnificent preservation obliges us to stop and contemplate this chamber carefully.

The third chamber where there is a large water font and whose entrances can be seen on either side was the room for relaxation, massage and dressing.

At the entrance in front of an old horse shoe shaped door we find the ablutions pool or fountain without its original covering; today it is in mock brick-work and very well preserved. Here was where they made their ablutions before going into the main building.

Let us not forget the great importance of the **baths** during the Spanish Arabic period where its practice was not only for social and hygienic reasons but also of great religious meaning. In Ronda there were several small baths in various parts of the town. We know of some from the records of the town distribution but it would appear from the remains preserved and also from its location that these were the main ones.

Looking around us we can appreciate, that because of all the remains here, we are in an area that had to be of great importance within the Islamic town. But what stands out are **the Ramparts and the gate of Xijara** from the XIth. century in the background.

On the death of Almansor, one of his lieutenants, making the most of the decline of the Caliphate of Cordoba, created the independent Taifa or kingdom of Banu Ifrán of Ronda. For forty years he governed his kingdom in peace and ordered the construction of buildings and walls such as the gate of Almocábar to the south or this one, called Xijara to defend himself from

Arab Baths

Rampart of the Jewis Quarter

the greed of the regulos or petty kings of the neighbouring Berber tribes.

This gate communicates the Lower district or Jewish Quarter with the town and is, together with the ramparts, the best preserved remains. It occupies an intermediate place between the first exterior wall of which four towers remain and this interior or main wall. From 1975 to date this part of the town has seen continual great improvements in the restoration and cleaning of architectural remains. The reconstructed gate is similar to the gate of Almocábar, with three arches, two horseshoe and one Gothic and an open space between the first gate and the second. Interesting also is the pavement of smoothed stones found in the main street during the restoration work carried out last Summer.

Let us once again take the down-hill path, the old entrance of the town, partly worked in stone and some rubblework. We cross the Arab Bridge and discover this picturesque **district of Mercadillo** whose charm we have seen since we first looked over the gorge.

Although it is possible that suburbs already existed in this northern part of the Madinat under Islamic domination, one thing is certain; that there was a Mozarab church, Church of the Oscuridad (or Darkness), and different Muslim sanctuaries thhroughout this aerea. It officially

became a district with its own status when Doña Margarita of Austria, widow of Don Juan, son of the Catholic Monarchs, returned her estate to the Crown when she left for Flanders in 1499 in order to become Governor there.

During that period there were great changes in the administration and government of the town. The new laws and salt taxes enforced on sales people and merchants on crossing through the gates made them stop coming into the town and instead they settled in places outside the walls. At the beginning they settled close to the gates, in front of the main gate of Almocábar and also in the northern area next to the Bridge Gate. Continual orders were made by the authorities to stop this abuse that caused damage to the Municipal resources and in 1512 an order was given by the Queen Doña Juana of Castilla

Dawn at Padre Jesús District

authorising the destruction of all the stalls and businesses outside the walls that did not contribute to the maintenance and defence of the town.

Peace and order were brought about successfully. The development of these districts outside the walls, today known as San Francisco and Padre Jesus saw the birth of a modern town with the construction of new urban centres and religious buildings for its new settlers. On the south side, in front of the main gate of Almocábar, all around the Hermitage of the Visitación, hundreds of huts, shops and traveller´s inns appeared.

On the north side the trades people settled on this open ground near the bridge and erected a chapel, rivalling the people settled in front of the Almocábar, and built **the church of Santa Cecilia**. Later it passed the category of parish church and today it is dedicated to Padre Jesús.

The church, as we have said, was originally dedicated to Santa Cecilia. On the construction of the New Bridge the majority of the population transferred to the top part of the Mercadillo which meant that this church was rather abandoned and so another more central church was built in the old convent of the Trinitarians Descalzos. This meant that Santa Cecilia was no longer the Mother Parish and so it became **the Parish of Padre Jesús.** It has a very popular statue

and the local people have a tremendous devotion to this image which is shown every Friday.

The façade-tower corresponds to the original building which was made at the end of the XVth. and beginning of the XVIth. century. Its Gothic stone doorway is crowned by a Renaissance bell tower with three semicircular arches. The church is not very large but it is well distributed and divided into three naves separated by two brick columns and two embedded columns on either side with capitals bordered with flowers in relief. These columns support six semicircular arches that make the central nave higher, with a beautiful Mudejar covered ceiling hidden by the restoration work of 1769 which was exuberant plaster work decoration that is still preserved. It is one of the most representative churches of local Baroque.

Many distinguished Rondans were baptized in this church, e.g. Vicente Espinel a man of letters, Ríos Rosas, the politician, and Cayetano Ordóñez "Niño de la Palma", who was a bullfighter. What`s more, very significant people from our society have been buried here; to name just one, Antonio Díaz Machuca the builder of the New Bridge.

The Fountain of Eight Spouts is in the centre of the square which has a very romantic XIX century air about it and so many films have been made in this area, such as the opera "Carmen" by Francesco Rosi in 1984, with our excellent tenor Plácido Domingo.

This fountain in Calle Real (Royal St.) evokes the glorious past of this district, first commercial and social centre of Christian Ronda until the middle of the XIX century. It is the only old fountain that has been preserved. It is made from stone with two fronts; one with eight spouts from which it gets its name and little rosettes make a frame around each one. The other side has a large drinking trough for the animals. This was made during the reign of Philip V at the same time as the gate which bears his name.

Walking up the street to the right we come across **the Convent of Madre de Dios** (Mother of God) built in the middle of the XVIth. century as a monastery for Dominican nuns. Mudejar elements mixed with Isabeline. Gothic and Renaissance abound throughout the interior of the convent.

The building is made around two large patios. We go into the first one from the same street as Santa Cecilia, across a great stone entrance with a semicircular arch and above it in the tympanum is the coat of arms of the Dominicans. An entrance of double arches leads us to the larger and more important patio. The lower floor has brick, semicircular arches and the top floor has basket-handled arches. Standing out on this floor are the Mudejar decorated doors which lead into the old Chapter House.

The church is built on one of the sides of the convent and we reach it from Calle Real.

It has just one nave with a half barrelled vault decorated in plaster with acanthus leaves, fruit and flowers that hide the original coffered ceiling of Mudejar style. Its semicircular entrance, also with the Dominican coat of arms in its tympanum, corresponds to mid XVII century.

Now the church belongs to Las Madres de los Desamparados de San José de la Montaña and the convent is now a school financed by the Unicaja Foundation of Ronda.

We continue uphill along Santa Cecilia street and although there is no sign to indicate it, nor are our eyes witness to any monument, be assured that behind those houses on the right and down a staircase we will discover one of the most delightful and least known corners of the Mercadillo area and at the same time one of the richest of our patrimony, **The Mozarabic Church of La Oscuridad.**

Situated in one of the old outskirts of the Muslim town it belongs to the district of La Oscuridad from which its name derives. Built from sand stone, it corresponds to the IXth. and Xth. century. It is of basilical style and despite having been looted several times we can appreciate, apart from the parroquial area used for liturgies and burials, it was also used by communities of hermits and monastics.

Let us continue uphill. Although we notice a certain hustle and bustle of people and vehicles, as if we were leaving the peace and quiet of the town behind us, it does not mean that this area we are in has no historical value. In front of us to the right the little shrine of Our Lady of Sorrows and at the end of this narrow street, to the left, **the Posada de**

Ocho Caños Fountain

City of Dreams

Las Animas. First we shall get to know the Posada or inn.

It is one of the oldest buildings of the Mercadillo area. It was constructed at the beginning of the XVIth. century and served its purpose as an inn right until the end of the XIXth.century. At the moment it is a home for elderly people.

The entrance is composed of a semi circular arch in stone and has a wrought iron balcony that has a small pediment with the symbol of Castille above it. In the past a statue of Our Lady of Souls (Animas) was there.

It gets its unusual name from the skull and bones over the door which symbolise the end of this life and the image from the pediment that represents Our Lady pulling souls out of Purgatory. She was the protector of early morning travellers and road workers.

It was an old inn as much for mule drivers as for knights passing through the town and it had the honour of housing the great writer Miguel de Cervantes y Saavedra during the period when he was a royal tax collector, and many other important personalities such as Richard Ford in the XIXth. century.

The distribution of this inn was discovered quite recently. It had a great stone-paved alley in the centre for horses to cross; on both sides were the rooms and bedrooms for the more wealthy and at the end, around the patio, the lofts, barns and stables for the animals and servants.

Let us retrace our steps in order to see the very interesting **shrine of Our Lady of Sorrows.**

Built in the time of Ferdinand VI in the year 1754 according to its inscription. This is the place where according to tradition, those who were condemned to death came to say their prayers before being executed in the square nearby during the XVIIth. and XVIIIth. century.

The chapel is rectangular in shape, covered by a roof with three slopes and profusely decorated with stone chippings of vegetal stalks that surround some medallions with paintings of the Evangelists.

On the front there is a little chamber in the shape of a small balcony with an altar piece of carved wood, and inside it is a statue of Our Lady of Sorrows. On both sides of the small altar are the heraldic arms of the Christian Monarchs and of King Philip V. On the inside is a hemispherical stone with

< Chapel of Our Lady of Sorrows   ∧ *Church of Socorro*   *San Francisco. Flea Market ∨*

Inn of Our Lady of Souls. Façade

the legend of the construction of the chapel.

But most original and noticeable are the two Ionic columns embedded with four anthromorfic figures in each one. They appear to emerge from sheaths and support the columns with a rope tied around their neck. Those on the inside have the appearance of bird men or fallen angels covered in feathers; the outer ones are human with social differentiation in their hair, their physique and also even in the thickness of the cords around their neck. These figures respond to the Manierist spirit of the XVIIIth. century.

At the top end of the street, **the Plaza and Church of Los Descalzos.** (Barefooted Carmelites) This is were the Rondans get together each year to commemorate the traditional feast of the eve of San Juan (or Fire Festival) and the beginning of the Summer Solstice.

The Church of the Carmelites, today Parish Church of Santa Cecilia, originally belonged to the monastic order of the Trinitarian Carmelites.

The church and convent were constructed by the Order in 1663 on top of the old Hermitage of Christ of Las Penas (Sorrows).

In 1836 the convent was closed and since then until now it has been a school, but in 1875 the church became the Parish of Santa Cecilia who is the patron saint of music.

It was restored some years ago. Its ground plan is in the shape of a Latin cross with three naves, the central one wider and covered by a barrelled vault which is decorated with vegetal elements and human heads, separated from the other two naves by thick columns with Corinthian pilasters that support heavy semicircular arches. Its transept is covered by a cupola which is decorated with

Tile from XVIII th. century. Salvatierra Palace

painted scenes of various Trinitarian saints and profuse Baroque plaster work.

The main façade is of sand stone and is composed of a semicircular arch decorated in leaves and vegetal motives and framed by Tuscan columns that support a split pediment with pyramids and balls above it. In the center is the Trinitarian coat of arms. The whole of the façade is in harmonising Baroque. It has a beautiful double set of split pediments in the centre of the façade with side balconies as in the doorway of the old convent. A well, raised above street level, closed by a thick grill of Rondan wrought-iron work completes the beautiful aspect of its entrance.

Now we shall cross over and take **the main street** which is named after **Vicente Espinel**. This pedestrian walk that continues down to the Plaza de Toros is the heart of the economy of Ronda, of our society and of our customs. It is a place for the elderly and the young to meet each other for a chat and to go shopping. These streets and adjoining plazas form the most important regional service centre for all the Serranía, (Mountain range). The street is from the XIX century and originated due to its being on the crossroads for Málaga, Granada and Sevilla-Cádiz. Some beautiful buildings and grills from the last century are evident.

Bullring. Façade

At the end of this street we observe in front of us a large esplanade, with lovely gardens, on top of the precipice and to the right of them the Bullring. This esplanade is the **Paseo (or Promenade) of Blas Infante.** Many people from Ronda will remember this place because **the Teatro Espinel** used to be here. The theatre(teatro)was built by the Modernist architect Santiago Sanguinetti,

Team of Horses. Contest in the Bullring

opened on the 20th. of May 1909 and ordered to be demolished the 15th. of April 1975. It clearly represented the middle class progress of Ronda in the early XX century where very important social events and modern history of Ronda took place. e.g. the first Georgista Spanish American Congress relating to the unique tax or later, in 1919, when the Andalusian coat of arms and green and white flag were created.

But the most representative building of all is **the Plaza de Toros (Bullring)** and a visit is a must. More a bullfighters sanctuary than a Bullring it is the oldest one in existence for modern bullfighting.

The entrance is very unusual, of neo-classical style but with some baroque detail, brought here at the beginning of the XX cen-

tury. It was originally on the front of the Blas Infante Promenade. It consists of a semicircular arch flanked by Tuscan columns that support a broken pediment with the coat of arms of the Real Maestranza (Royal Institute) and an elegant balcony of wrought iron with allusive bullfighting motives.

The plaza forms a complete circle with double arcades of depressed arches on 136 Tuscan columns. The royal box stands out as its decoration is more profuse and its columns are fluted.

It was inaugurated the11th. of May 1784, but some of the rows collapsed during the celebrations and it had to be reconstructed and was inaugurated once again the following year during the May fair with the performance of Pedro Romero and his rival Pepe Hillo. José Martín Aldehuela who at that time was occupied with the construction of the New Bridge, worked on the reconstruction.

It has 5.000 seats and its ring is 66 mts. diametre and is the only bullring with stone barrier. The bullpen gate, the presidential box and the royal box are situated on the same side of the building. All the seating area is completely covered. As you can see this is a very unusual bullring.

It was constructed by and belongs to the Real Cuerpo de la Maestranza de Caballería de Ronda, (Royal Corps of the Institute of Knights of Ronda) whose history goes back to the Catholic Monarchs, at the end of the XV century as Brotherhood of the Holy Spirit. King Felipe II in the year 1571 had the old

Bullring of The Royal Corps of the Institute of Knights of Ronda

Goya's Etchings. Pedro Romero

brotherhoods reorganised and changed into Royal Institutes. The Brotherhood of Ronda was the first to obey this Royal warrant and it was legalised in 1572, becoming the first and oldest Royal Institute of Spain.

This Brotherhood was entrusted with the military education of the nobility, in horse riding and in the use of weapons with tournaments, jousting, bullfighting and other military exercises, always with the idea of keeping their pupils active and to have them prepared for duty when requested by the king. Since it was founded the Real Maestranza has been responsible for numerous military deeds.

Bullring. Goyesca Bullfight. September

Ronda is charm

But let us return to the bullring which was the first enclosed for bullfighting on foot and the cradle of modern bullfighting. At present very few bullfights are held here but in the second week of September the Goyesca Bullfight and the Ronda Bullfight of Lances are held. The Goyesca Corrida is unique in the world according to Ernest Hemingway, and aficionados from all over the globe come to receive lessons in Classical Bullfighting and many of those attending dress in the style of late XVIII th.century period of the artist Goya. The celebrations are in memory of Pedro Romero who according to all chronicles gave life to and settle all the rules for modern bullfighting.

He was born in Ronda in 1755. He came into the bullfighting world at the age of eight, retired when he was seventy two, and died at the age of ninety without having been gored by a bulls horn despite the fact that he had killed almost 6.000 bulls face to face, and not as Pepe Hillo his rival of that time "a volapie" (method of killing a bull in which the matador runs at the stationary animal and drives the blade between the shoulder blades).
King Fernando VII named him Director of the newly created Sevillian school and Founder of the Rondan school of bullfighting.

He inherited his interest in tauromachy since the nobility stopped bullfighting on horseback in the open squares and bullfighting on foot by local professionals became popular.

His grandfather, Don Francisco Romero, began as one of the bravest men of his time by standing in front of the bull with a hat in his hand or a cape, just as a pastime, but he became so expert that he began to teach how to use the cape and to kill by the rules he had

Cayetano Ordóñez, Ernest Hemingway and Antonio Ordóñez. (Foto Martín), 1959

ment and on the keystone of the arch there are two coats of arms of the Real Maestranza crowned with three stone pinnacles. It is now the entrance of the recently created Riding School of the Royal Institute of Knights of Ronda.

We cross the street called Virgen de la Paz. In front of us the charming pedestrian street of Pedro Romero, full of restaurants and bars and at the end of it **the Plaza del Socorro** with its church and lots of children running about and playing.

After the War of Independence, many of the streets and squares in Ronda were dilapidated and impassable so it was decided to improve and embellish all the area between Plaza del Socorro and Plaza de la Merced. All the houses with the circle and the cross over the doors built by Pedro Romero in what is now Calle Marina and those that have since disappeared from Calle Virgen de la Paz corresponded to that period.

There is a fountain in Plaza del Socorro; pathways have been made and trees planted for relaxation of the Rondans in wintertime and at the end of the XIX century a large building which was to become the Casino or Artists Circle close up on the north side of the square. The square is rebuilt in 1994 and an underground parking is made, managing to recuperate the original charm and open space for which it was originally intended.

acquired from his own experience. He invented the muleta, a scarlet cape with a wooden stick for support, used by the matador to kill the bull face to face, putting himself in front of his crew.

His father, Juan Romero, was the one who really organised the cuadrilla (or crew) with picadors, banderillos, assistants, etc. He died aged 102.

Let us leave this edifice which is a must for aficionados and novices of the beautiful art of the bullfighting world, but not before visiting **the Taurine museum** so that from its many interesting exhibits we can learn more about this noble art of tauromachy. A leather waistcoat from the XVIII century or the jet black suit of lights worn by Joselito "Gallito" on the death of his mother or some of the costumes with influence from the period of Goya and worn by the master Antonio Ordóñez, apart from a very wide collection of Goyescan costumes and suits of lights of the best bullfighters from this century. It is a permanent exhibition and dedicated to the two great Rondan dynasties, the Romeros and the Ordóñez.

On the way out there is another stone doorway which opens out to the horses´ patio or Riding School of the bullring. It is more Baroque than the main part of the building. On the pedi-

Orson Welles and Antonio Ordóñez. (Foto Cuso), 1964

But the most important building is **the Church of Socorro.** The early hermitage was built on top of the ruins of an Islamic worship place or sanctuary where ascetics, devoted to pious habits lived, and on top of what used to be the Royal residence of the Master of Calatrava during the conquest of the town. To the original construction a lazaret was added and finally at the end of the XVI century a hospital for the poor and pilgrims which received the name Socorro (Succour). At the beginning of the XVII century the hermitage was demolished and in its place a new church was built and opened its doors for worship in 1709. In 1836 it was established as a parish church and subsequently in 1936 it was destroyed.

Antonio Ordóñez' Costume. Goyesca Bullfight. Bullring Museum

The actual building is of a new ground plan and was constructed in 1956. It is square with three covered naves with five domes and a rich baroque decoration in plaster work. The façade is flanked by two quadrangular towers crowned by little tiled roofs and beautiful local wrought iron balconies. Its stone doorway with semicircular arch has a split pediment above it with a little niche containing an image of the Baby Jesus in the centre which reminds us of the façade of the old church which no longer exists. In its tympanum there is a very large Imperial coat of arms. In conclusion it is a neo-baroque church which is very representative of the political time of its construction.

We leave the Plaza del Socorro and taking the Marina Street and Niño Street we arrive at the **Plaza de la Merced** where before our eyes we see the majestic **Church-convent of La Merced.**

It was founded as a convent, devoted to Our Lady of Mercy in the year 1551, but the church, which was not built until the end

of the XVI century, is all that is actually left. The use of the building by the Mercedarian Order was suppressed in 1822 as by then the number of monks had diminished to such an extent that they could no longer survive. It immediately became a barracks until 1846 when it was bought privately.

After the Portuguese revolution in 1910 the Carmelite Sisters of Olivais, Portugal, take refuge in Spain, bringing with them a relic, the left hand of their founder, **St. Teresa of Jesús**.

Afterwards, the 15th. of October 1924, the Carmelo of Ronda is founded with the intention of bringing together all the Portuguese nuns scattered across Spain. During the Civil War the relic is requested by the local Committee and later it appears in Málaga where it is given to General Franco who keeps it until his death in 1975. Once again in the convent of Ronda it is today the object of great local devotion.

The church is of Manieristic - Mudejar style. It has three naves although only the central one, covered by a coffered vault with

Goyesca Bullfight

lunettes and fascias is fit for use as the side naves are today blocked up and converted into cells and living quarters for the Carmelite Community.

A hemispherical dome above a drum with little windows covering a transept and the chancel above a great basket handled arch at the bottom of the church are the most important factors in the interior, after the restoration of the XVIII century when the Mudejar coffered ceiling was lost.

The façade is made from rubblework and mock brickwork, from which emerges its octagonal side tower with angular pilasters that have openings for the bells. Its doorway with semicircular arch stands out. Above it is a niche which contains the figure of the founder of the order, St. Peter Nolasco. It has a split pediment with the Mercedarian Orders´ coat of arms.

Another very important reason for visiting this convent is for the quality of the local confectionery made and sold daily by the Carmelites.

For a few moments let us leave churches and convents and enjoy a place which for many Rondan generations has been the reminiscence of childhood for our parents and grandparents; the fluttering of young wings ready for flight in the spring of youth and the mature satisfaction of watching our children and grandchildren running about. Divine Dawn of Life accompanied by the rustle of the leaves on the trees, stirred by the breeze from the Tajo and restrained by the music of the fountains. Many dusks have caressed our faces with the tenuous smoothness of the sunsets of San Cristóbal, and many awakenings to flattery have become enriched with the most beautiful picture that nature has been able to offer us from these gardens of **the Alameda del Tajo (Promenade of the Gorge).**

At the entrance, the monument by the artist Vicente Bolós, resident in Ronda, to Don Pedro Romero on the bicentenary of the birth of such an illustrious Rondan. With his right hand the maestro appears to be saying and showing us the first rule of the art of Bullfighting "Stop" but in reality what he is saying is "Go slowly, very slowly. You are going to discover at the bottom, where the gorge is 178 mts. deep, the most perfect union between man and divinity".

The Alameda was made on what used to be the esplanade of the common land of the market place in front of the convent of La Merced in 1787 by the Mayor, the Marquis of

Iron Works as an art

Pejas. It was finished and improved in 1806 by Vicente Cano who was mayor also but was ridiculed by the town with the nickname *"The thirteen by thirteen"*. It was said that he was such a voluminous man that he weighed 13 arrobas and 13 lbs (1 arroba = 13 1bs) which is approximately 150 kilos and as the saying goes "He enjoyed good health".

In order to complete the works, which are the envy and admiration of all who visit us, public funds were not used. Instead it was paid through fines imposed on those who hurled obscene insults, were foul mouthed or scandalous in public places.

The brilliant idea of the Mayor, due to the detriment of the flippancy and informality of the people in their everyday conversation not only obtained enough money but what is more it contributed to the construction of a great square, today Plaza de España, between the New Bridge and the Plaza de Toros (which were newly built) so that the neighbours had a place to stroll under its spacious galleries.

The completion of the Alameda of San Carlos (name which was given to it on its inauguration and called so until recently) gave us a great green open space in the very heart

v *Gardens of Cuenca City.*

The Hanging City

Gardens of the Gorge ^

of the market place, measuring 178 mts. long by 77 mts. wide; very diminished recently with the construction of the Espinel Theatre (1992) and the Culture House; but its privileged position right on the edge of the precipice with its varied species and quantities of flowers and its numerous fountains, its wrought iron lamps, comfortable stone seats and well situated balconies make it one of the most beautiful and well proportioned promenades in Spain.

We leave the Alameda del Tajo from the interior; by the bottom gate on the left. We continue along the back of the Plaza de Toros, as far as the gardens of Blas Infante, and walk straight towards the enormous building of the Parador (one of the state owned hotels). There, an open iron gate allows us to pass the dining room of the hotel until we reach the café of the building, where, from the terrace, we can appreciate the indescribable beauty of the city with its suspended houses and its old mills in the bottom of the abyss. Now we can understand why Ernest Hemmingway makes a beautiful description of this wonderful place in his novel "Death in the Afternoon".

We reach **the Plaza de España** with the west side of the New Bridge and the challenge of the old city always with us and in the centre we see the monument in memory of the Rondan, Don Antonio de los Ríos y Rosas. Illustrious tribune and honourable politician. He became a member of the Spanish Parliament, Minister and President of Congress in the year 1862. He was the first member of a very great saga of Rondans, as his nephew Don Francisco Giner de los Ríos (1839 - 1915) Master of liberal intellectualism and creator of the Free Institution of Education or his grand nephew Don Fernando de Ríos (1879 -1949) Minister of Public Education, of Justice and of State during the Second Republic and Ambassador to the United States during the Civil War.

Now, slowly, we shall continue our walk towards the district of San Francisco. We cross the new bridge and take Armiñán St.; a modern road that crosses the town from north to south and gives a certain respite to the traffic that circulates nowadays. The Magistrates Court, the back of the City Hall and the old walls of the Castle occupy the right hand side of the road as far as the slope of Las Imagines (The Images) where the remains of the old Gate of Mancebias and a splendid view of the Mercadillo, to the left, give way to **the Church of the Espiritu Santo** (The Holy Spirit). A building which appears to be waiting for us in order to say that in the shadows of its walls we are going

Bullring.Aerial View

Square of Spain. Ríos Rosas Monument >

Light and colour

to know one of the most beautiful and loved districts of the town of Ronda.

Fernando the Catholic King had the Church built on top of the ruins of the mosque which was in the Arrabal Alto (the higher suburbs) next to the tower of Ochavas. An Almohad octagonal tower that defended this natural access to the town, and was destroyed by the Christian lombards during the conquest. It was consecrated under the advocation of the Holy Spirit in commemoration of the day in which the town was taken; a day which, that year, coincided with Whitsuntide .

One can easily see by its sober and austere construction that it was built during the time of the reconquest of the Kingdom of Granada. It was completed in 1505, the year Queen Isabel died. For a time it carried out the functions of the Main Church while work of Santa María was being completed.

The edifice is of great homogeneity and is of Gothic style with some Renaissance influence. It has just one nave which is 30 mts. long and 9 mts. wide, which is divided into two sections by a great triumphal semicircular arch that is supported by thick, raised pillars which are incrusted into the walls.

In the first section, through the triumphal arch, there is an apse covered later by a great Renaissance dome with two arched blind windows. The front of the church is occupied by the main altar which is baroque and covers practically all the central apse with a painting, above it of the Arrival of the Holy Spirit and in the centre another one on wood of the Virgin of La Antigua in beautiful Byzantine style. Above the high altar there are three coats of arms worked in stone; two of them belong to Friar Bernardo Manrique, in whose Bishopric they were made and the other one is the Imperial coat of arms of the House of Austria. On the Epistle side we find the door with its semicircular arch that leads to the sacristy.

On both sides of the great triumphal arch there are two side chapels of semicircular arches and ground vaults which conform to the transept of the church. In the Epistle chapel there is a baroque altar dedicated to Our Lady of Fatima, which has a small niche with a statue of San Cayetano, and in the Evangelists chapel we find the altar of the Sacred Heart of Jesus with the beautiful urn of the Holy Burial of Christ, which is carried out every year on Good Friday together with the statue of his Mother, Our Lady of Solitude.

In the second section, at the end of the nave, the chancel raised by an interesting basket-handled arch that reminds us of its homonymous in the church of the Royal Monastery in the Escorial and next to the entrance door of the chancel a little museum with walnut furniture carved beautifully in Rondan style, baptismal books and other objects of historical interest.

Its simple façade has a pediment finished off with a small round window in the centre and a semicircular arched door. Above the arch is a small niche with the Holy Spirit in the shape of a dove.

We leave the church and at the side of the entrance ramp is the delightful chapel with its geometrical ceramics of the patron saint of this district of San Francisco. We continue down the street with its old fashioned Rondan air, and at the end of it we catch a glimpse of **the gate of Almocábar.**

This gate takes its name from the Arab word "Al-maqâbir" or Gate of the Cemetery as it is near the main necropolis, outside the city, according to Islamic tradition. It was the main gate and gave access to the Barrio Alto (top district) which is today called Holy Spirit, and to the Muslim market town crossing the Gate of the Imágines (since disappeared) which had a drawbridge and a portcullis.

As you can see it is on the south side where the walls are high and strong as it was the least naturally protected area. It was built at the end of the XIIIth. century, beginning of the XIVth., between two large semicircular rubblework towers with three consecutive arches; the end ones being horseshoe-shaped and the centre one Gothic with a high opening for the portcullis or grill that protected the gate.

In the middle of the XVIth. century, during the time of Charles I another main access part was added to the front. The ground plan was quadrangular and its main gate was crenellated in Renaissance style, which, after its restoration in 1965 was transferred to the left side. It consists of a semicircular arch in stone, above which is a large royal coat of arms with the Imperial Eagle.

Worth mentioning, apart from the grandeur of its medieval ramparts, are the projectiles in stone used by the Christian lombards encrusted into the towers forming crucifixes which signify the return of the town to the Christian faith as a result of the Conquest. In the same way, because of its quaint and picturesque air and because of the connotations with the traditions of this quarter we should observe the drinking trough called "El Pilar" next to the gate. It is the beginning of a Royal stream and a place for older generations to meet and chat. But never about new events!

On crossing through the gates the whole aspect changes, physically and in concept, although many families today have moved over to this haven of peace and cordiality of **the San Francisco District**. This open space in front of the ramparts and main gates of Ronda has had many important uses since its historic foundation. The Romans used it as an exercise ground for its equestrian order. After, the Arabs made their public cemetery at the end of the esplanade and used the rest of the ground as a **Musalla** (where they held great religious celebrations) and as a **Musara** (a place for equestrian exercises and for public diversion). Finally it was used as an enclosure for training nobility in the noble art of horse riding after the Christian conquest.

In this square of San Francisco, where the monument commemorating the birthplace of Pedro Romero is situated, we find the **Church of Nuestra Señora de Gracia** (Our Lady of Grace) which is the first newly-built church in Ronda. At the beginning it was in the very centre of the actual square, devoted to Our Lady of the Visitation (or the Ascension) and

Genal Valley. Júzcar

∧ *Holy Spirit Church.*

San Francisco District.

Ramparts of Almocábar. ∨

transferred later to the side, which is its present position and now under the advocation of Our Lady of Grace, patron saint of the Real Maestranza de Caballeria de Ronda (Royal Institute of Knights).

The Real Maestranza abandoned the church in the XVIIIth. century which left it neglected and forgotten during the past centuries to date. It is a very simple church with one nave that has a high barrelled vault. At the end there is a wooden Baroque alcove with a square ground plan. It has polychrome floral decorations. A commemorative stone on the main altar tells us that its construction was started in 1507 and completed in 1538.

Just across the square, scene of the Sunday morning market and of numerous establishments were one can try our typical sausage cooked in wine, we have **the Convent of the Franciscans** under the patronage of St. Joseph.

The convent was built on the property of Francisco Robledo y Ríos in the year 1664 during the reign of Philip IV of Spain. It now belongs to the Order of the Franciscanas Descalzas (The Barefooted Franciscans) under

the rule of St. Clare. The edifice, after the restoration in the XVIIIth. century, is of late Baroque with two patios and an interesting room which was originally the dormitories of the convent. The church has one nave, and a barrelled vault with lunettes and fascias and a great profusion of decorative geometric mouldings and trimmed plaques. Its simple stone doorway, with a semicircular arch between pilasters is crowned by a pediment in the centre of which there is a coat of arms of the order and a Franciscan cross.

Now, taking the street of San Francisco, which occupies practically all the area once used as the old Muslim necropolis, we arrive at **the Convent of San Francisco,** the building which gives its name to all of this district.

It is one of the convents founded by the Catholic Monarchs, after the Christian conquest, to commemorate the place where the royal residence of King Ferdinand was situated during the siege of the town of Ronda. It was built at the beginning of the XVIth. century, in the year 1505, it is a hybrid of Gothic-Mudejar, although it is at present a modern building used as a boarding school, as

Almocábar and Charles V Gates

it suffered a great deal of damage during the War of Independence and also during our Civil War.

The most representative is its church of a Latin cross whose Mudejar coffered ceiling was destroyed by a fire and substituted recently by a modern one; but what is really preserved in this building is its stone door-way in the most pure and unique Isabeline style in Ronda. It is composed of an tented arch with fine borders decorated in laurel leaves with intertwining stalks and leaves of thistle, surrounded by the Franciscan cord, where the emblem of the order lies, and on the sides, inclined, are the coats of arms of the Dávilas and of the Ovalles, original patrons of this convent.

We can rest or continue, but perhaps it would be better to dedicate an afternoon to the **Cave Church of Our Lady of La Cabeza** which is almost a moral obligation during our visit of Ronda.

Following the road to Algeciras, when there are no more buildings of the San Francisco District, at the Pila (or fountain) of Doña Gaspara, we take a lane to the right which is about 2 Kms. long, passing olives and pines, that takes us to the favourite place of the poet Rilke on his walks while he lived in Ronda.

On arrival to this clearing we feel an intoxicating sensation as we contemplate Ronda in the distance as if the earth had given birth to it, after the pain and grief of its gorge in the

Ronda is tradition

Guadelevin river. The New Bridge, majestic, is our witness to the many poets and artists that come here, drawn by the delicate breeze at dusk that our town exudes. The house occupied by the British painter, David Bomberg, during his two long stays in Ronda, indicates to us that the lane on the right, worked in stone, will take us to the church.

A whitewashed room in front of the delightful baroque chapel of the XVIIIth. century tells us about the Virgen of La Cabeza. An image of great popular devotion that for a long time was taken out in the processions as patron saint of Ronda, and which now, is the reason for a great pilgrimage every year on the second Sunday of June, when many Rondans surround the Virgin in order to transfer her from Ronda.

The rupestrian church of La Oscuridad (Darkness) was referred to during our visit of the old market place, and now we have, before us, the second of those mozarabic churches used by the Christian community of Ronda during the Islamic domination .

It was excavated out of calcareous land from the Tertiary period between the IXth. and Xth. century. It is formed by a group of naves, hollowed out of the bare rock, of which we can appreciate two sections. One dedicated to

Church of Our Lady of La Cabeza

Rupestrian Church Virgen de la Cabeza. Interior

EXCURSION THROUGH OUR SERRANÍA OR MOUNTAIN RANGE.

Your stay in Ronda can be extended for as long as you wish. Not only the monumental visit can take several days, but the surrounding district and the region can prolong your holiday into several weeks. The historical-monumental collection of Ronda, complemented by the natural parks of the Serrania, and the white villages of the area are, today, one of the most complete and charming offers throughout Europe.

To meticulously detail all the opportunities available for the visitor would be to compose such a heavy informative compendium and there would be no surprises. What is more delightful than to be able to lose oneself and discover beautiful corners on one´s own? So please allow me, dear Reader, to continue with some interesting places and itineraries, in my humble opinion, and leave others for you to discover for yourself.

The first route we are going to take is easily done. It is relaxing; through countryside and olive groves, with here and there a splash of white farms and small cottages, and from time to time a herd of Iberian pigs amongst the holm oaks and cork trees or perhaps a flock of sheep and goats would accompany us along the road-side. This is a route which will show us how life is in our agricultural villages with the cordiality and informality that is peculiar to them.

We now take the Campillos road and on leaving Ronda we turn left towards **Arriate.** Its name originates from an Arab hamlet called "Arriadh" which means orchard. It is a municipality since 1661 and at the moment has a population of 3.450. It is a village which is loved by all and its inhabitants are recognised as being very hard working. It has become a very industrious and productive village, well known for

worship and the other to monastic dwellings.

The main section, dedicated to worship, consists of one central nave with a semicircular apse that finishes in a triumphal semicircular arch, where the main altar is situated, and three naves at right angles to it. The sacristy has some niches cut from the rock which hold statues of devotion, and under the main altar is the entrance to a crypt, but due to its limited size it would appear that it was used for keeping relics rather than for burial. The part corresponding to living quarters is a clear example of a monastery made to be lived in by a community, organised with cells, kitchens and communal areas.

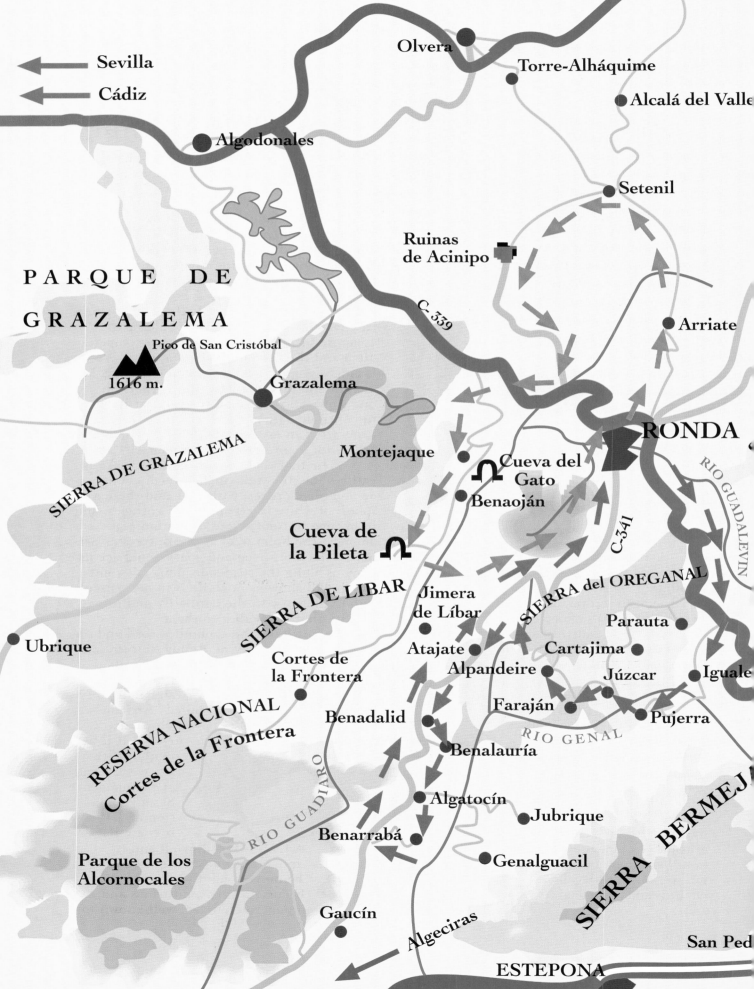

Serranía de Ronda

Sevilla

Cádiz

Olvera

Torre-Alháquime

Alcalá del Valle

Algodonales

Setenil

Ruinas de Acinipo

C-339

Arriate

PARQUE DE GRAZALEMA

Pico de San Cristóbal

1616 m.

Grazalema

RONDA

RIO GUADALEVIN

SIERRA DE GRAZALEMA

Montejaque

Cueva del Gato

Benaoján

Cueva de la Pileta

C-341

SIERRA del OREGANAL

SIERRA DE LIBAR

Jimera de Líbar

Parauta

Ubrique

Atajate

Cartajima

Júzcar

Iguale

Cortes de la Frontera

Alpandeire

Farajeán

Pujerra

RESERVA NACIONAL
Cortes de la Frontera

Benadalid

Benalauría

RIO GENAL

RIO GUADIARO

Algatocín

Jubrique

Parque de los Alcornocales

Benarrabá

Genalguacil

SIERRA BERMEJ

Gaucín

Algeciras

San Ped

ESTEPONA

Genal Valley

its pork sausages, the beautiful furniture made by excellent craftsmen and for the production of olive oil.

The villagers will invite you at any time to enjoy the tranquillity and the local products. It is a village which knows how to enjoy life and to express its gaiety as few other villages in the region. Its fiestas are worth knowing, such as Los Campanilleros or Auroros which is when they sing to the Virgin Mary on Sundays, during Holy Week or the Patronal fiesta of St. Peter on the 29th. of June, apart from the famous fiesta called Partir la Vieja on the first day of Lent.

We leave the village of Arriate, to continue through the Rondan districts of Cimada and Los Prados until we come to the boundaries of the province of Málaga and enter the province of Cádiz where we come across the unusual village of Setenil.

In front of us in the distance, like a white dove resting on the hills is the village of **Olvera** with its 8.721 inhabitants. An old seigniory of the Dukes of Osuna, it became a strategic point during the reconquest as a frontier town between Lower and Higher Andalusia, as its fortified castle proves.

Many Andaluces make a pilgrimage to this village, not so much to see its magnificent neo-classical parish church which was completed in the middle of the XIXth. century, but to its sanctuary dedicated to the miraculous patron saint, La Virgen de los Remedios.(Our Lady of Consolation) on the outskirts of the town.

But we are really heading for **Setenil or Setenil de Las Bodegas,** considered to be a regal village by the Catholic Monarchs

with 3.316 inhabitants. Situated just inside the province of Cádiz and surrounded by the province of Málaga and extensive groves of holm oaks, it was built on top of a Miocenic hillside and gives the impression of sliding down into the River Guadalporcún.

It is an elevated village, defended by solid ramparts whose history developed together with that of Ronda and its district. It was conquered with great effort by the Catholic Monarchs in September 1484. In the parish church is a chasuble donated by Isabel the Catholic Queen to commemorate such a joyous occasion.

In this fascinating village, where entire streets are built under the overhanging rocks whose humidity makes them slippery, we come across its caves - old, fresh and deep cellars converted into unusual white houses encrusted into the rock that invite us to make a detailed and memorable visit of such a unique village.

We continue along the road which goes towards the village of Gastor, Balcony of Andalusia, and soon we will find on our left the detour that will take us to the town of **Acinipo**, whose Roman theatre will guide us to its location.

Acinipo, Land of the Wine, or Old Ronda as it is affectionately known by people, is situated at 800 mts. above sea level, in the heart of Roman Andalusia and which according to Pliny and Ptolemy belonged to Celtic Baeturia. It became a municipal district with power to mint its own coins with the legend of Acinipo and a bunch of grapes together with two wheat ears and later its inhabitants obtained the same rights as any citizen of Imperial Rome until it became

completely rural at the beginning of the Vth. century.

At the entrance, Iberian remains, recently discovered, belonging to a settlement of the Bronze period from the VIIIth. and VIIth century B.C. encourage us to continue our walk across mounds of stones and taegulae up to the highest part of the plateau where we find the most representative and best preserved construction, The Theatre.

Situated in the most western part of the ruins and at the very edge of the precipice that protects the town in this area we find its tiers worked in stone as in Greek theatres, using the gradient of the land to make stairs to go up and down to the last seats. Following, at the bottom, the orchestra

covered with great slabs of red marble and finally the stage made with great hewn stones that has three entrances to the stage with three niches above them to place statues of gods or tribunes. Some rooms for musicians, actors and storerooms complement the good preservation of this construction and the possibility of it being put to good use with the minimum of work.

We commence our return journey but now we turn to the right which will leave us on the main road that brings us to Ronda from Seville.

Once again we turn to the right and within about four kms. we find, to the left, a sign which indicates the way to Montejaque-Benaoján. We drive on through a beautiful forest of gall oaks, with the

Olvera, like a white dove

empty reservoir of Montejaque and the entrance to **the Cave of Hundidero**, which forms part of and communicates with the famous Cueva del Gato (Cave of the Cat). We continue as far as Montejaque.

The village of **Montejaque** is connected to the Hacho Mountain range and as its name suggests, the Lost Mountain. It is a chain of white houses which are regularly whitewashed, clinging to the side of the mountain.

It is of Arab origin and used to be an estate of the Count of Benavente. There are at present, approximately 950 inhabitants and its emigration has been one of the most important social phenomena of the last decades. Its great prestige in the production of deviates from the Iberian pig and its first steps as a place of leisure and tranquillity for select tourism has converted it into a desirable place for short holidays.

Leaving the village we go around the other side of the hill of Mures until we reach the village of **Benaoján** which was originally Arabic and whose name means "The Baker's House". There is a population of approximately 1.600 and it was also a seigniory of the Count of Benavente. It is an industrious town where the production of pork sausage which is well commercialized, together with livestock, especially pig

Setenil

breeding are the main resources. Its railway station which is next to the river is just two kms. away and is the cause of an incipient tourist industry.

But we are going to take the route which passes through the northern side of the village and after approximately four kms. travelling through crevices and crags we reach the Pantheon of Andalusia's Prehistory which is the **Cave of Pileta.**

Situated on the north side of the Sierra of Libar in the solid rock of the Mestas, it

Acinipo

Cave of the Gato

was discovered in the year 1905 by Don José Bullón Lobato, a shepherd of the region. Then in 1911 it was visited by an English man, Colonel Vernet, who, through various publications in the English press put it on the map. Then, in 1912 it was examined by the experts Mr.Breuil and Mr. Obermaier who published and talked about its great prehistoric value. It was declared a National Monument in 1924.

Through its majestic limestone chambers, narrow corridors and passageways we discover fabulous figures created by nature that harmonise with the stalagmites and stalactites; and in the chambers of The Bats, The Serpents, The Moorish Queen, The Castle, The Cathedral, The Dead Woman,

The Fish, The Waterfall, The Great Chasm, The Organ or The Sanctuary...we can admire rupestral paintings of incalculable value in ochre, yellow and black and some in red and yellow which are approximately between 15,000 and 20,000 years old.

But above all the Cathedral of Prehistory owes its fame to the extraordinary paintings and drawings in the Sanctuary Chamber and in the Fish Chamber.

The Sanctuary Chamber stands out more than any other part of the cave for the perfection of its paintings. Apart from two human figures and numerous symbols, fourteen Palaeolithic representations (of the Solutré period, found also in France) exist and of which the pregnant mare is the most expressive. No less important is the Chamber of the Fish, the most spectacular for all who visit it. It is large, with many black schematic symbols from the Neolithic Age with a clear magical-religious feeling, where the most emblematic drawing in the cave is found "El Pez" (The Fish). It is painted in black with charcoal and measures 150 cm. long x 80 cm. wide and is the most significant Palaeolithic painting in this prehistoric sanctuary; what is more, within its outline is the drawing of a seal, and surrounding it numerous animals are represented.

This cave is actually in the **Natural Park of the Sierra of Grazalema**, one of the three parks that are found in the Rondan mountain range, and one more reason to stay a little longer in our region.

Situated in the most western part of our mountain range, it was declared a Biospherical Reserve by UNESCO in 1977

Caves of "La Pileta"

Like a dream. Pujerra Village >

Popular Museum. Benalauría

and Natural Park in 1984. It has a very unusual characteristic: it is the place with the highest rainfall in Spain with an average of 2.200 mm. per year and as in the Park of Las Nieves we find the sylvan variety of the Tertian period called Abies Pinsapo Boissier. A rugged landscape full of holm oaks, cork trees, gall oaks and vetches interspersed by scrub, such as rockrose, gorse, and medicinal plants such as oregano or lavender; populated by deer, fox and genet; apart from having one of the most numerous colonies of tawny vultures in Spain. All this will give us the pleasure of programming an exclusive excursion to visit the Park which we can complement with a visit to the village of Grazalema, the most symbolic of all the so called Pueblos Blancos (White Villages) in the province of Cádiz.

But we have to return and so once again we take the Benaoján road and on reaching the village we turn to the right in order to continue in the direction of Ronda by the road that goes along the River Guadiaro. We pass the railway station and see on our left the entrance to **La Cueva del Gato.** Cultivated land and farmsteads accompany us until we reach the military complex of the Fourth Regiment of the Spanish Legion. Finally the Ronda-Seville road. Now we turn right and within two kms. we are back were we started, in the town of Ronda.

EXCURSION THROUGH THE GENAL VALLEY.

This new route is along the road leading to the Costa del Sol in the direction of San Pedro de Alcántara, a road which was restored in 1980 and which is now the main tourist entrance to Ronda.

We continue along it with the impressive lime-stone masses of Sierra Hidalga with Melequetín and Oreganal, and in the background the Torrecilla of the Sierra de Las Nieves. At 1.919 mts. it is the highest point of our mountain range and of the province of Málaga.

The Park of Sierra de Las Nieves is formed by this mountainous complex of thick woods and rich vegetation. The visit to the park will be very gratifying and will make at least one more day excursion. To reach it, all you have to do is continue along the road until you reach km. number 13, turn left and follow the sign for Rajete, whose track, in good condition, will leave you at the Refuge House of Fuenfría. From there you will be able to visit, comfortably, on foot, all of the Park.

It was declared a Natural Park in 1989 and recently a Biospherical Reserve by UNESCO. You will find a visit to it a very interesting and instructive experience and you will

also discover the greatest extension of Pinsapo Abies Boissier of Southern Europe. As we have already said in the Natural Park of the Sierra of Grazalema this is an arboreal species of the tertiary period, or simply a very primitive tree and endemic to the Iberian peninsula. You will also enjoy the splendid forests of gall oaks, chestnuts, pines and ash and other interesting members of the coniferous family such as the yew, but always accompanied by aromatic plants typical of these mountains, such as rockrose, rosemary and thyme.

From the highest point, the Torrecilla (1.919 mts.) you will enjoy an impressive view of the Costa del Sol, from Gibraltar to Fuengirola. On clear days you will distinguish the Rif chain in North Africa. The silence of the environment will be broken by the majestic flight of the royal eagle or by the furtive fluttering of the wings of a sparrow hawk or peregrine falcon which are so plentiful in these environs. Numerous herds of common goats and one or two mountain goats and roe deer will delight you during your walks in the park where

View of the Serranía

The Genal Valley. Atajate

the chance meeting with one or two foxes, mongoose or wild cat will complete an unforgettable day in this heavenly spot of our mountain range.

But we should continue on our way for our second excursion that as you will see could be extended to a third or fourth but I shall leave that to your own decision. But always remember that in this delightful valley you will find a series of tourist services in almost all of its villages, such as restaurants, rural houses, farmhouses, hostels and refuges, situated in privileged places

Sunset

always totally respecting the local culture and its environs.

Some ten kms. from Ronda, in the direction of the Costa del Sol we take a right turn leading towards Igualeja. We penetrate into some arid limestone hills where the road becomes narrower. We continue and all of a sudden a panorama of reds, yellows and greens opens up before us, with a little white village in the background which appears to be sliding down its familiar cliffs. It is **Cartajima**. The town of Cartajima we should say because it was given this distinction by King Fernando VII. Surrounded by woodlands of chestnuts, holm oaks and cork oak groves it has a population of some 325 inhabitants and it almost completely depends on the production of timber and the commercialisation of chestnuts.

The village which now appears before our eyes is **Igualeja**. The village is well known in our region as being hard working and fun loving and because the source of the River Genal is just outside it, and this is what configures the valley which we are about to know, one of the few natural paradises still preserved in Andalusia.

Its origin is Berber as is the case with most of the villages in these mountains. According to the historian Ibn Harm "To the region of Ronda and Valley of Genal came the Walhasa, tribes from the mountains of North Africa with an Arab minority". It was always connected with the history of Ronda as part of the province of

Tacoronna and as part of the seignory of Prince Juan after the reconquest.

With a prosperous population of approximately 1.100 dedicated mainly to the production of pork, chestnuts and handicraft activities it has always been considered as a hard working village that multiplies its population by four during its very famous dramatic representations of the Passion of Christ during Holy Week. The celebrations of the feast of St.Gregory, the patron saint, at the end of August, and the fiesta of the Toro de Fuego (The Bull of Fire) are some of the many attractions for visiting this village.

Let us continue. This narrow road which leads to Pujerra invites us to stop frequently to contemplate its hundred year old chestnut trees. There are six kms. of loving care and attention scattered over these thick woods right up to the village.

Pujerra is a white pearl in the middle of a thick chestnut wood. There are approximately 320 inhabitants who, like many of the neighbours of the villages in this region, are dedicated to the exploitation of its woods, and to the incipient breeding of pigs and goats. They have now opened some tourist establishments in an attempt at developing and at the same time maintaining the simple charm of this village.

We go back towards Igualeja. At about two kms. we see that, to the left of the road, there is a great, surfaced, forest track leading to the village of Júzcar, which is in very good condition for traffic and goes as far as the banks of the River Genal. Its profound silence is only broken by the smooth water

of a newly born crystalline brook which is later to become a great river. During its course it waters the numerous market gardens that have appeared on its banks whereas before it used to operate the many water mills that filled its banks.

We make our way to Júzcar and stop on route to say good-bye to Pujerra and to contemplate in the distance, as if it were hanging in mid-air, the village of **Jubrique**.

The exploitation of the chestnut and the cultivation of its numerous market gardens watered by the Genal, apart from the breeding of some pigs and goats, are the main resources of its almost 900 inhabitants. A village which in the distance looks more like a white spot of lime amongst trees and cotton, had, in its period of splendour, wineries, liquor factories and mining. Now it is involved with the rest of the villages of the environs in the commercialisation and export of chestnuts. Its historic importance in the Valley of Genal is endorsed by its church of San Francisco which used to be an Arab mosque.

We arrive at **Júzcar.** It is a small village like Pujerra with about 250 inhabitants and covers an area of approximately 33.66 sq.kms. dedicated also to the cultivation of chestnuts, vegetables, olives and vines. The Royal Factory of Tinplate was installed within its boundaries during the reign of Philip V at the beginning of the XVIIIth. century.

Great vines used to cover all the hills of the right side of the Genal until the phylloxera blight appeared at the end of the XIXth. century. The production of wines and

Benadalid

liqueurs were the most important resources of the majority of these villages in the past. Now, we can enjoy in any of them an exquisite "mosto" (new wine) during the months of November and December, accompanied, naturally, by the best products of the Iberian pig and goat´s milk cheese in olive oil.

We continue towards the left until we reach the village of **Faraján** or Delightful as its name means in Arabic. The landscape appears to change; the thick chestnut woods are replaced by a much more mountainous area of brushwood and rockrose where pig and goat breeding abounds. The population of approximately 315 is dedicated basically to the harvesting of chestnuts and to livestock breeding; this being a good place to enjoy good Serrano ham and some delicious home cooking. Faraján must have been very rich and important within this area judging by its many religious buildings still preserved: the Church of Our Lady of the Rosary from the beginning of the XVIth. century, the Church of Saint Sebastian, the Hermitage of the Holy Child or the Carmelite Convent.

We continue our excursion taking the road towards **Alpandeire**. We notice that the landscape we have become accustomed to, comes to an end. We have left behind the green and reddish chestnut woods for the white and grey limestone; from the wooded fertility to the dry, barren land.

Alpandeire is a town because that title was granted by King Fernando VII. It has a very large church which is the parish of San Antonio. The parish is from the XVIth. century and was restored two centuries later. It stands out like a big cathedral within the humble urbanism that surrounds it. The town has some 320 inhabitants who live from goat and pig breeding and from poor agriculture. In addition to this, as it was the birthplace of the miraculous **Capuchin, Friar Leopoldo of Alpandeire**, many of his faithful make pilgrimages to the area. It is a beautiful place to stroll through its narrow streets and stop in the square to contemplate, in the distance, the chain of white villages that are all part of the Genal Valley.

We come out of the town which was one of the first villages to be established by the Arabs in this Serrania and immediately, in the middle of a dry and barren landscape, to the left, we see a sign which indicates the house, Villafría, where Friar Leopoldo lived.

It has been a brusque change. Winding bends across a bare environment take us right up to the hillside of the Sierra de los Perdigones (young partridges) where we have the cross-roads of the main Ronda-Algeciras road. If we turn to the right we will be in Ronda immediately but as the wise would continue, we are going to turn left towards Algeciras in order to see more of the best kept treasure of our mountains which are the villages of the Genal Valley.

The presence of a shepherd and crows in flight across arid and tortuous terrain covered in gorse, rockrose and chaparro are

Alpandeire

the only concordant notes for us until we reach the smallest village in the province of Malaga.

Atajate has only 150 inhabitants but it used to have a castle and was a very important village on the Algeciras-Gibraltar route to Ronda and in the interior of the peninsula. Its great Fiesta del Mosto at the end of November, is an invitation to visit this tranquil spot during those days, but its production of home made bread and typical sweets of almond loaf are an obvious temptation to stop in this place at any time.

We continue along the road and once again see the different greens that we have missed in the last kilometres. Fig trees, olives, poplars and white houses are our travel companions again and away in the distance are the dense woods of the Genal Valley.

The road evens out and **Benadalid** with its emblematic castle appears. At one time the seigniory of the Count of Feria, it now has a population of approximately 270. Its name in Arabic means "Sons of Jalid" who were Berber warriors from Africa that settled in this region. From that period the castle, which like many others, defended the area around it, still exists, but now it is used as a cemetery. In addition there is an attractive church from the XVIIIth. century.

Very interesting are its fiestas of Moors and Christians which are held during the feast of its patron saint- Isidoro - at the end of August; its Crosses of May and its

Genal River

Corpus procession. But you should get to know Benadalid inside out.

We return to the road again and stop just as we leave the village in order to contemplate this white village with its earth coloured tiles, enlarged by its castle, clinging to the foothills of the mountain of the same name. Its serene beauty is an image that will stay engraved in our minds.

Continuing, in three kms. we take, on the left, a detour that will lead us to the village of **Benalauría.** Two kilometres of narrow road surrounded by a dense vegetation of chestnuts, olives, almonds and holm oaks until we reach a heavenly place of strong Arabic influence with its white walls and steep, narrow streets.

There is a population of approximately 580 which was totally dedicated to the

exploitation of its woods of holm oaks, cork oaks and the cultivation of vines. Now it has turned to rural tourism with rustic houses for rent, with a restaurant and an ethnic museum installed in an old olive oil mill. The craftsmanship of cork and heather wood are some of its new resources.

We must go back. To leave this heavenly valley is not easy. We could carry on and continue visiting some of the villages that are left for us to discover, such as **Genalguacil, Algatocín** or **Benarrabá,** and even **the National Park of Los Alcornocales** that is not so far from here. But that decision is for you to take and could be the reason for other excursions through our Serranía.

Cayetano Ordóñez "Niño de la Palma" and Antonio Ordóñez. Monuments. September, 1996. Foto Cuso